Daryll Scott has managed something startling ᴛᴏ ᴍᴇ — ɪɴ a ꜱᴛʀᴏɴɢ clear voice, he has developed a description of the New Code NLP patterning that he has worked diligently to master – the patterning developed by Carmen Bostic St Clair and myself – that is fresh and quite distinct from what I would have proposed.

It strikes me as working very nicely for the specific application that Daryll has in mind – namely, an introductory book on the New Code NLP that is designed primarily for business people. There are many differences of perception that I could point to that distinguishes Daryll's perceptions about New Code NLP from my own however the point here is NOT uniformity but getting the message into the business community in an effective form. And in this, I judge Daryll's efforts to be very effective.

I welcome his contribution to the growing movement to position New Code NLP in the business community and in the larger context.

John Grinder
Co-creator of Neuro-Linguistic Programming (NLP)
Creator of New Code NLP
Bonny Doon, California

When I started working with John Grinder and Carmen Bostic St Clair, we sought to initiate higher standards in the field of Neuro Linguistic Programming. This led us to design and deliver a completely new 'Trainers Training' and launching the ITA. Daryll Scott, I am pleased to say is one of the gifted people who is member of the ITA and is an innovative trainer and writer who is bringing the latest NLP ideas to the business field. In *Can we Start Again?*, Daryll lays out NLP patterning in a way that enables readers from different backgrounds to learn NLP applications that will be of enormous value in improving performance across a range of business activities.

Michael Carroll
ITA Co-Founder
Founder NLP Academy
NLP Master Trainer

For a complete list of Management Books 2000 titles
visit our web-site on http://www.mb2000.com

CAN WE START AGAIN?

The Patterns & Techniques of
Neuro-Linguistic Programming
applied to business presentations
and interactions

Daryll Scott

2000

First published in 2006 by Management Books 2000 Ltd
Forge House, Limes Road
Kemble, Cirencester
Gloucestershire, GL7 6AD, UK
Tel: 0044 (0) 1285 771441
Fax: 0044 (0) 1285 771055
Email: info@mb2000.com
Web: www.mb2000.com

British Library Cataloguing in Publication Data is available

IBN 9781852525460

Acknowledgements

There are many people that I would like to thank for their contribution to this 'accidental' project. They include:

Michelle Rhodes for an excellent introduction to NLP.

Carmen Bostic St Clair for challenging a group of NLP trainers to be flexible and creative in getting The New Code out there.

Martine Snow, Craig Killick, Jo Harris, Anthony Denton and Dominic Scott for their support and encouragement.

Hiran Ilangantileke and Arton Baleci for valuable feedback – metaphoric and specific respectively.

My wife Helen for her continued, unswerving belief in my every endeavour.

My parents for providing a childhood environment where flexibility and unconventional thinking were encouraged.

Dr John Grinder for the extraordinary and unexpected level of guidance, challenge and support - I am humbled by his genius and grateful for his attention.

I would like to dedicate this book to my business partner Ben Houghton for his support and the many hours spent provoking and eliciting from me this presentation of the patterns of NLP. Without Ben, this book would not have happened.

For Joseph

Contents

Introduction **11**
    Starting out *11*
    The dreaded question… *12*
    So why am I reading this book? What's it all about? *15*
    How should I work through this book? *20*
    So what's the big idea? *21*
    As if. *24*

1. The Science Bit **31**
    How real is real? *44*
    All we can experience is FA *46*
    This does not make sense……yet *47*
    Getting yourself in a 'state' *54*
    Summary *61*

2. Making a Connection **63**
    How are you getting on? *65*
    My kind of people… *66*
    What are you looking for? *70*
    Did you see it? *75*
    How do you do it? *76*
    Sudoku? *77*
    What does it mean? *78*
    I see what you are saying… *80*
    Lost in Translation *84*
    Answer the question… *85*
    Spell Check; Language Check; Send. *86*
    What do I do with this? *88*
    What I need to see/talk about/get is. *89*
    Homework *89*
    Summary *92*

3. Body language **93**
   An interesting topic *95*
   VAK Physiology *99*
   Handy tricks *99*

4. Investigative Listening **103**
   Are words a blessing or a curse? *105*
   Are you a Mind Reader? *116*
   There's a lot going on... ....*120*
   Why? Because... ....*128*
   Another way of unpacking it. *140*
   The Farrelly Model *141*
   Summing up *145*

5. Influential Speaking **147**
   What is influential speaking? *149*
   To pre-frame this chapter *150*
   Framing your communication. *151*
   The Milton Model. *162*
   The upside-down Meta Model. *165*
   Putting it together *183*
   Summary *184*

6. Negotiation **185**
   One 'chunk' at a time. *191*
   Chunking Questions *195*
   A Negotiation model *197*
   Summary *200*

7. Presentations **201**
   School Days *203*
   Utilization *204*
   Not my style. *204*
   What are they thinking? *205*
   How can you talk to everyone? *207*
   Delivery. *213*

8. Self Application **215**
   Re-visiting the map. *217*
   We can start again! *217*

So where do you think you're going? *218*
How will you know when you get there? *219*
Watch out for the story teller....................................*221*
Another Point of View...*223*
What prevents you?..*226*
Check your own attribution of meaning.....................*226*
Question your own modal operators...........................*227*
Add options *227*
Listen to your own advice? *228*
Coaching Behavioural Change....................................*229*
Moving on...*234*

Bibliography.. **235**

Introduction

Starting out

I don't know if you have had the experience of learning to drive. If not, perhaps you can imagine what it might be like...

I remember the morning of my first driving lesson. It was my 17th birthday.

It was a bright July morning, the cloudless sky was a beautiful bright blue colour and the street outside was quiet. I sat in the comfortable chair next to the living room window and watched the empty street, listening for the driving instructor's car. My knee bounced with a nervous excitement, I could hardly contain the enthusiastic energy I was feeling as the driving instructor's car came into view.

My driving lessons were a birthday gift from my parents and for some time, like many teenage boys, learning to drive had become the most important thing in my life. I would talk about driving at any opportunity. I was aware of every 'L' plate on the road (and there were so many of them at the time). My every attention was on learning to drive and the feeling of freedom that I had attached to it.

The first ten minutes of the lesson were a kind of introduction to the controls of the vehicle and the conditions of the lessons, what I would do, what the instructor would do, how that would work and a few possible scenarios as examples.

Then I was able to set off slowly, swerving from left to right with the engine screaming and the car lurching forwards as if attempting to vomit out its engine.

There was so much to remember and do all at once – it felt impossible, and awkward. I found it difficult to imagine ever being able to drive a car effortlessly.

It occurs to me now that at no point before setting off on our journey did the instructor say, "Which roads will you be driving on?"

When you learn to drive, the intention is that you reach a level of competence so that you can drive on any road. Most roads have very similar rules, so when you become a competent driver the method is universal.

The thing that enables us to become competent to drive on any road is the ability to make the activity of driving unconscious. You no longer have to be mindful of what gear you are in, where the pedals are, which pedal does what, where the indicator is. You just drive, without thinking about it consciously, so you are able to pay attention to the road and other motorists.

When you have passed your driving test, you need to take your first journey alone. For most of us, that journey begins at home and we drive off down a familiar road that we have driven many times.

It's very easy to use what we have been taught because we are in the environment where our teaching was applied. We know exactly what to do, without thinking about it.

It may be a few days before we find ourselves on an unfamiliar road and our skills are put to the test. By this time our competence at driving without an instructor has increased – and new challenges are relatively few compared to the number of familiar roads, so it's possible for our competence to grow steadily – we can apply our skills to our new challenges one 'bite' at a time.

As you learn to drive down many roads in your future, you can notice that your attention is on your vehicle; here and now. The destination will take care of itself – it will be wherever you are if ever you decide to stop.

The dreaded question...

Welcome to this book. As you are reading this page I know that you have many questions, and one of them may even be the dreaded question.

Since embarking upon my NLP journey, the only question that I do not enjoy hearing is, *"What is NLP?"*

It causes a paralysis in my mind. It's an overwhelming feeling. I think: *Where do I start?*

John Grinder (the co-creator of NLP) might say something along the lines of:

NLP is a modelling science that sets out to discover what makes the difference between the performance of a genius and the performance of an average performer within the same field. This is achieved by unconscious assimilation of the genius' behaviour (suspending any attempt to consciously understand), through imitation of micro muscle movement, until the modeller can produce the same results as the subject in the same time or less. Each element implicit in the patterns of modelled behaviour is then isolated and removed to see if its omission makes a difference to the results. The behaviour is then coded that the tacit ability of the genius can be made explicit.

This process has left behind a variety of patterns and techniques that are extremely empowering to the individual. Carmen Bostic St Clair (who currently works with John Grinder furthering the development of New Code NLP) offers a great, practical definition of NLP application:

"It's a different way of seeing, hearing, feeling and thinking about the world that provides flexibility and choice."

Although these definitions are both valid, it is possible that, within your current frame of reference, you may feel 'none the wiser'. You may perhaps be confused by the definitions as you do not currently have any experience that will allow you to 'make sense' of them. How does NLP relate to your life? What's in it for you? If you are familiar with NLP, I'm sure that you can appreciate how the first-time reader will have difficulty attributing meaning or concrete experience to either of these definitions.

I don't know what led you to this point, when you are about to invest your time in an amazing journey. Whatever it was, I'm fairly sure that it was something more than a concise and accurate definition.

Maybe you have witnessed a friend or colleague making positive changes to their performance, career, lifestyle and communication. Perhaps you have enjoyed a presentation on NLP or met a trainer who has provided some insight or left you feeling intrigued. You may have seen Tony Robbins or heard about Derren Brown's 'mind tricks' on television or something else entirely and made the decision to experience this extraordinary and easily accessible science for yourself.

Perhaps my difficulty in answering the dreaded question is caused by the fact that I care a bit too much about the outcome of the conversation; I'm rigid about what is an acceptable outcome and consequently my communication becomes inflexible. I have seen a lot of people free themselves of some personal limitations, heard the difference in the effectiveness of their communication, and I would like as many people as possible to have that experience. I am therefore keen to communicate this amazing, empowering technique as effectively as possible.

These days I tend not to answer the question. Instead I ask what is the intention in asking it. I will then ask what the person has seen, heard and experienced in the past. Only then do I have a frame of reference to begin to discuss this potentially enormous subject.

Based on their answers, I go on to provide either reasons, definitions demonstrations, or effects and consequences.

This often provides a frame of reference where the listener is able to attribute some meaning to NLP having not actually experienced it yet. However, in being more specific, I am focusing on just one area/pattern/application of NLP, and thus excluding several others.

At best the listener will have a small amount of awareness of just a pattern of NLP.

My approach of restricting the definition of NLP in order to make it easier for the listener to attribute some kind of meaning within their current frame of reference is common within the field. Many people believe they know what NLP is, and in truth they do not... yet.

The patterns of NLP are not NLP.

They are the product of the NLP modelling process, the tracks that two intrepid explorers left in the snow.

The subject matter of this book is what many people understand to be NLP, but that's not entirely accurate. The subject is in fact just some of the techniques and patterns that have been coded *as a result of* the NLP modelling process in an applied context.

To define NLP as being these techniques and patterns is as absurd as defining the science of physics as a television. If someone with no subject knowledge asks, "What is physics?" you are unlikely to describe a television *(or some other example of the application of physics)*.

It is hypothesis and experimentation within the field of physics that lead to observing the effects of certain things and constructing the explanatory principles, 'laws' or 'rules' that seem to govern them. These discoveries can be implemented to invent a television.

In terms of this analogy, NLP is similar to physics, and the modelled patterns and techniques of NLP are similar to the discoveries. These patterns and techniques can have many contextual applications (like the TV). NLP in the context of business is just one possible application – the television.

So why am I reading this book? What's it all about?

In writing this book I am operating on the assumption that you are reading it for one of three reasons:

1. You are interested in the field of NLP and want to read about it in a way that will be useful and easy to apply in your professional life.

2. You are working through this book in preparation for an 'NLP Practitioner for Business' training course.

3. You already have knowledge and experience of NLP and would like to see if you can gain more perspective or gather a few extra resources from reading some familiar content in a commercially applied context.

For the purpose of clarity I would like to address each of the three reader-types in turn. You may read the one most applicable to you or enjoy reading through all three.

1. Dear business professional:

Welcome to the world of NLP. My intention in writing this book is to provide a practical introduction to NLP, by putting the material across in an accessible and instantly usable way. There are a lot of books on NLP. This book aims to present the subject in such a way that you can make immediate use of what you learn. It's practical, simple, and it works.

In addition, the content of the book is broken down into 'application topics' that clearly indicate the possible commercial outcomes that you will gain from successful implementation of the techniques and patterns. They are:

Making a connection

We all know how important the ability to connect with other people can be in every area of our individual lives. "It's not what you know, it's who you know." Any business activity can be made easier or more difficult by your ability to communicate with others, and the more positive a connection you make, the easier the communication becomes. Think of a difficult type of communication that you deal with in your day-to-day life. Now imagine having the same difficulty if the person you are communicating with is your best friend. Even if the topic or message is difficult, the process of communication becomes easier and more effective if there is a 'rapport' between the individuals involved. Would you like to learn how to create rapport with everyone almost immediately?

Body language

It is suggested that 55% of meaning comes from our body language. (Like most statistics, I have no idea how this can be analysed as a precise and universally correct statistic. However it is obvious that the meaning of a word can be completely changed by the gesture that accompanies it.). When I tell people that NLP includes an awareness of body language they are usually very interested. For many people, body language is a fascinating subject, yet few take the time to study it. What can happen when you are able to use your body language to create an agreeable atmosphere between yourself and another person? How useful could it be to be able read others' non-verbal signals?

Investigative listening

Many of the senior executives and directors who I have worked with have said to me something along the lines of, "One thing that I wish I had learnt to do earlier in my career is to listen." When you are listening, the moment you think 'I know where they are going with this', or begin thinking of what you are going to say next as a reply, your ability to listen is diminished. This is how many misunderstandings happen. How often do misunderstandings happen in your daily life? Would you like to develop the ability to listen more precisely to what is being said, and more importantly, what is not being said?

Influential speaking

Have you ever found yourself saying the words, "That's not what I meant"? Have you got some way into a conversation and said, "Hang on, can we start again?" Allow me to ask you a question. Is anyone ever motivated just because you have told them that they should be? Are you ever confronted with people who have 'already made up their mind' about what you are discussing? Would you like to learn language patterns that bypass resistance and engage the listener, utilising their motives and reasons, making your messages more agreeable and influential?

Presentations

In today's working environments, delivering presentations is becoming a larger part of our everyday working lives. We are all aware that there are different 'personality types', and that people like to experience things in different ways and have different learning styles. However, we have a tendency to explain things the way we understand them, and if people don't 'get it' we explain them again the same way (maybe slightly slower or louder). How beneficial will it be when you can structure presentations, proposals and messages in a way that engage all personality types and learning styles?

Negotiation

Almost every interaction is a negotiation: sales conversations, managing your supply chain, interacting and allocating tasks and responsibilities on a day-to-day basis, everything where there is flexibility and more than one possible outcome. Without flexibility it's not a negotiation; it's a battle of wills, or an argument. Before arranging a Friday night out with my friends, I will have a negotiation with my wife. How useful will it be when you can identify the parameters of a negotiation and explore mutually beneficial outcomes, doing deals that will remain positive into the future, maintaining agreement and influence throughout the process?

Self application

NLP is often associated with goal-setting. We know that setting well formed objectives can be very helpful in getting what we want. As well as setting the right kind of (SMART) goals, how can you make your objectives more believable and compelling in your own mind? How can you identify what currently prevents you? What are the limitations you put on yourself? Would you like to reframe your own thought processes, and perceive things differently?

In delivering the patterns in such an applied context I trust that it will make the patterns easier for you to experience and more applicable to your everyday life and career. I hope that this experience of NLP in an applied context will encourage you to take it further.

2. Dear future practitioner of NLP in business:

If you are attending one of my courses, or someone else's that takes a similar approach, the intention is that you will learn patterns and techniques which will enrich your lives by providing you with more flexibility and choice.

I am primarily concerned with your ability to actually do it, to use the techniques in your everyday life – and you can.

I have met several clever people who can explain NLP, and their 'textbook' knowledge is probably better than mine, yet they do not 'do' NLP. They have not applied what they have learned to themselves and they only use their skills in 'NLP environments' such as practice groups.

I can think of several reasons for this, based upon my understanding of learning styles, the 'state' of the individuals during the learning experience and personal limitations preventing experimentation or utilisation. However, these are only a few possible reasons, and I would never claim to *know* 'why' another person thinks in a particular way. For now, I am simply working with the fact that I have observed several people go through NLP Practitioner courses with a variety of results after the course.

In embarking upon an applied Practitioner for Business course, you can learn the powerful patterns of NLP in real contexts, even utilising specific situations in your business life, to dramatically change the results you get. The patterns and techniques you will encounter are framed in realistic scenarios so that, as much as possible through this limited media, you can actually experience the patterns quickly and easily.

I am currently experimenting with the belief that; learning and experiencing the patterns framed in everyday scenarios will allow you to use them more frequently and therefore quickly reach a degree of unconscious competence.

I have excluded some of the patterns that comprise an NLP certification from this workbook, simply because, in my opinion, a book is not the best way to learn them.

To be explicit, this book addresses some presuppositions of NLP, representation systems, the Meta model, most of the Milton model,

18

logical levels and chunking. There is also some material dealing with linguistic framing and reframing, physiology and 'state'. The book does not include sub-modalities, anchoring or any other change patterns. These are best experienced on your course.

3. Dear NLP practitioner, master practitioner or trainer:

You are already familiar with Neuro-Linguistic Programming, so allow me to pre-frame this book. I don't know if you are a practitioner, a master practitioner or even a trainer of NLP, but whatever the case, perhaps you can take a moment to think of the contexts in which the subject is typically delivered. I know that you know that NLP can be applied to any context, any situation and any type of interaction. I would then ask, how often *is it* applied?

Between my Master Practitioner and Trainer certification I was fortunate enough to spend several weeks assisting on NLP trainings with someone that I consider to be a very good trainer. As well as reinforcing my own learning through repetition and experience, I was able to objectively observe a variety of people embark upon their journey into the world of NLP. I had the additional advantage of knowing some of these people outside the training environment, mainly through business, so I would be able to observe the results of the training after the course. It was these observations that compelled me to treat the topic the way I now do.

My observation of the people who I am familiar with was that, although they had a great experience, and made many positive changes as a result of experiencing NLP techniques, and demonstrated a promising level of competence within the training environment, they returned to everyday life and immediately reverted to previous behaviours. I'm sure the positive changes stayed with them, yet in some cases the competences of language and flexibility of thought evaporated with the change in environment.

So what happened? The trainer had done a great job within the training environment. Why did the skills not transfer across into everyday life? Some were able to achieve this – why not all of them? It is reasonable to assume that people will have different experiences, and take different things from their experiences, and perhaps different people will be in a different state of readiness to take some of the ideas on board.

I've also noticed that it requires an intuitive leap to take the patterns and techniques from the context in which they experience them, and apply them to their everyday lives. Some people do this effectively, others not as much.

I would like to stress that this is an opinion rather than a fact. It is based upon my perception of people's competences. It is not measurable; it may not even be true, so I'm not prepared to present it as a statement of fact. I would invite you to apply it to your own experiences and see if you feel that there is any truth in it. Take it or leave it – I don't mind either way. If this does strike a chord with you, then I would encourage you to read on…

I am aware that, by being more specific about the context in which the patterns and techniques are used there is a possibility that I am restricting or limiting the model. I am happy to accept this consequence at introductory or practitioner level in return for a higher level of self application and competence in the context of everyday working life.

Besides, I think there is an element of this 'bias' that happens within a more conventional delivery of NLP anyway. The patterns and techniques are delivered within the context that John and Richard discovered them – Therapy. So just ask yourself, what percentage of people who finish an NLP Practitioner are motivated to use their skills in therapeutic change work whether as a career choice or part-time interest? In my opinion it's a wonderful thing to apply your skills to – and it is the most obvious application. Does that prevent some people from looking for further creative, alternative applications for this amazing science? Think about it…

This book uses metaphors and examples that are applied to everyday business life, explicitly pointing out the commercial advantages of the application of NLP techniques and patterns.

If you train or use NLP in business, this book can be a valuable resource for the application of what you already know. Please enjoy it for what it is.

How should I work through this book?

From start to finish. In order to structure this book I have assumed you will read the chapters in order. Many of the later chapters refer to ideas, techniques and patterns covered in earlier sections. It will also be advantageous if you take time to pause at the places where it is indicated to do so.

My intention was to write this book in a style that comes across as if I am talking to you, so that it is as experiential as possible. I hope this is how you are reading it.

Lastly, rather than simply read and consciously evaluate this book, I would invite you to experience it as much as possible. At several points within the book you will be asked to imagine, think of an example of, or do, what is being described. The more you do this, the more you will get from the material.

> *Tell me and I'll forget*
> *Show me and I'll remember*
> *Involve me and I'll understand*
> Chinese proverb

So what's the big idea?

As you work your way through this book you will find it punctuated with what I have called 'big ideas'. These ideas are indicated in the text by a thought-bubble illustration. They are the 'presuppositions of NLP' – assumptions you can make that will increase your flexibility of thought and behaviour. You can increase your effectiveness as a communicator in business, or as a business practitioner of NLP, by taking on these ideas.

These ideas are like beliefs that you can choose to operate from.

I use the words 'beliefs' with caution. I am not suggesting that you should believe these big ideas, or anything else for that matter, simply because I suggest that you do so. Instead, try them on. Experiment with them. Act as if they are true and see what happens. Then ask yourself, "Are they useful? Do they work?"

These big ideas, presuppositions, convenient and empowering assumptions, are the thought patterns employed by the most flexible and effective communicators.

The big ideas are the product of studying or modelling several geniuses that achieved amazing results in their field.

21

Are they true? I don't know. It's not important to me whether they are 'true' or not.

Do they work? In my experience, yes!

When you begin to operate from these beliefs, your communication and personal interaction will become far more effective.

You can just use these beliefs in certain situations, or employ them in every area of your life. What's important is that you notice the results you get when you use them.

So, to provide you with an example, we will cover the first, and for many people the most challenging big rule here and now:

Cause or Effect

Can you think of people who, when describing their career or current situation, speak as if everything has been caused by someone else, or something beyond their control?

It's not their fault. There is nothing that they could have done about it. People always treat them like this. It always just happens.

Does thinking in this way help people to find the answer to their challenges?

If you consider an event to be nothing to do with you, are you addressing how it happened and how to get different results in the future? Or are you are writing it off as 'beyond your control'?

In addition, I would ask you to begin to consider that everything that happens to you was, in an important sense, caused or created by you. Even when you do not act, your lack of action will have an effect. In some way or other, perhaps we cause almost everything that happens to us?

To make it easier to accept, think of it this way for a moment:

In any given situation, if we had behaved differently, the outcome would be different. True?

Therefore, our behaviour has created our outcome, surely. At the very least we have provided the opportunity for it to happen.

Allow me to provide a few examples to think about.

When I take on a new coaching client, I am often provided with a brief from an HR or learning and development person describing the behaviour of the person I will be coaching. They describe how this behaviour has been noted by many people and is a cause for concern in some way. I then meet the individual and find no evidence of the behaviour.

I'm sure that the behaviour exists in certain contexts, yet the way I behave, the way I communicate, my attitude, my approach, my beliefs, or something else, is different and the negative behaviour does not happen. I get different results.

How is this possible?

If I were to say to the person giving me the brief that they were somehow fuelling the negative behaviour they would disagree. They would say, "I was very professional in giving feedback," or, "It's not just me, he's like it with everyone." "Everyone says this about him."

Yet I am getting different results. If it were beyond their control, surely it would also be beyond my control?

Here's a different example:

I was recently stuck in a traffic jam on a motorway. I was on my way to a meeting so I phoned ahead and explained that I would be late and could not say how late. There was nothing I could do about the traffic, or being late, so I sat back, listened to the radio, reflected on a project that I was working on and thought about what to get my wife for her birthday.

After a while my attention drifted to the person in the car next to me. He was red-faced and white-knuckled as he gripped the steering wheel and stared intently ahead focusing on the number plate in front. I could see that his breathing was quick and shallow. He was in a stressed 'state'.

If you asked this person, he would say that the cause of the stress was the traffic jam; as if it were not something he was doing; as if he had no choice but to be stressed.

I was sitting next to him, in the same situation, feeling relaxed. How is this possible? If the traffic jam causes stress, surely I would be stressed as well.

From my perspective it was very easy to see that the stress was something that he was doing to himself. He was running an internal process that I was not. He was creating the stress, not the traffic.

The traffic does not cause him to be stressed; his reaction to the traffic does, and it is possible to react differently.

Another way of thinking about this is to consider that you are choosing your responses to a stimulus and creating the effect.

If you are thinking of a situation and wondering, "Did I really create this?" ask yourself if this situation, or something similar, is a recurring pattern in your life or career. Has something similar happened in the past? If you are getting the same results again and again, then would it be safe to assume that it's something to do with you?

If you always do what you have always done you will always get what you have always got.

An empowering first step in this NLP journey would be for you to take responsibility for the results that you are getting and recognise that you have choice – it is possible to behave differently.

Only when you take responsibility can you begin to evaluate your own behaviour, and add choice and flexibility to change the results that you get.

As if...

In the previous section entitled 'what's the big idea?' there was a suggestion to act as if these resourceful ways of thinking are true. (By 'resourceful' I mean 'acting as a powerful resource' – a use of the word which I will repeat throughout the book.)

This is an important point and I would like to be more explicit as to why.

Let's imagine you are reading this book and you are presented with a new idea. You quickly run the idea through your neurology and accept it or reject it. You are basing this decision upon your existing knowledge, experience and prejudices.

For many people there's nothing wrong with this process. Although it prohibits you from having the flexibility of thought to effectively evaluate or generate a new idea. You are not giving the new idea a chance.

When you are operating from your existing beliefs, you are unable to accept new and valuable ideas that are in conflict with those beliefs. You may even go into a defensive behaviour to protect the old beliefs.

Only by letting go of your old beliefs, just temporarily if need be, can you adopt a new or alternative approach and truly evaluate it based upon the results you get.

To demonstrate this, I would like to draw upon some famous words from one of the most flexible thinkers the world has ever known.

Albert Einstein said, *"We can't solve problems by using the same kind of thinking we used when we created them."*

In order to find new resources, a new perspective is required. If you continue to do the same mental processes, you will continue to get the same results.

This is fairly obvious, so why don't we change our thinking when we are getting unwanted results. What prevents us from being able to have this flexibility of thought?

Could it be that beliefs and things that we consider to be facts limit us? Do they set rules and boundaries around what we are observing?

Let's imagine that I provided you with an unusual looking item and said, "What fruit is this?"

You study the surface of the item and then cut it open, observing the colour and the pips or seeds inside. You then refer to your encyclopaedia of fruit and find some fruits that are similar in some characteristics but not the same.

You are likely to have concluded one of a few of things. Perhaps you would find the fruit description closest to it and say that's what it is. Or you would decide it was a new undiscovered fruit. Or you would think that you were unable to correctly identify it. Or you would think your encyclopaedia had omitted a type of fruit.

The real answer is that the item is a vegetable. Now you may have come to that conclusion anyway, but my point is that believing the item to be a fruit would prevent you from correctly identifying it. Only when you let go of the belief that it's a fruit can you begin to have the perspective that it could be something else and add the resource of a vegetable encyclopaedia.

We are limited by our 'facts' and 'beliefs'. Maybe most of your facts and beliefs are true, I don't know and I'm certainly not interested in challenging them; I have no idea what they are. However, if you believe them to be true and do not let go of them in order to check that they are true you are limiting yourself. You will be continuing to use the fruit encyclopaedia.

Einstein said: *"The only thing that interferes with my learning is my education."*

I'm not sure if he was referring only to his formal education, but this limitation is true of any explicit knowledge.

An illustration of this that is particularly relevant to Einstein's quote is the field of Quantum Physics.

Quantum theory has been described as the most successful set of ideas ever devised by human beings. It explains everything from the periodic table of the elements and why chemical reactions take place to the stability of DNA and how alpha particles tunnel out of the nucleus. Quantum theory is essentially mathematical and has never failed in practice.

The theory is non-intuitive and defies common sense, so in the early days it was easier to explain quantum theory to an absolute beginner than to a classical physicist.

The problem is that classical physicists were so absolutely certain of their ideas and theories, having had them confirmed for many years by careful detailed experiments. In their minds, the theories had become facts.

We all have the ability to take an idea and, if it is adequately proven to us in practice, make it a factual reality, thus creating a barrier in our minds with which to deflect anything that does not conform to this belief. In doing so, we are limiting ourselves.

So what can you do about this? If it is your intention to expand your world then I suggest you develop the ability to take on an idea, and behave as if it is true, in order to evaluate the effects and consequences of operating from that mindset.

The alternative is to evaluate everything from your existing frame of reference, which provides no opportunity for growth as you are not challenging yourself or doing anything differently.

How can you know if a new idea is right or wrong without trying it? How can you say what a pair of shoes will feel like until you try them on? So the two questions I would encourage you to ask of anything you discover are:

1.   Does it work – yes or no?
2.   What are the effects or consequences of this?

Then I suggest that you exercise your free thinking. By operating this way you will be evaluating ideas and beliefs on their consequences rather than your existing knowledge and experience.

We tend to set up 'filters' to make sense of our experience and the world around us. Our 'facts' or 'beliefs' are filters. When provided with new information we tend to make it fit within the conditions of these filters and reject anything that does not get through. If you wish to continue running everything new through your existing 'filters', then what do you expect to get from this book?

During the past few years I have encountered many misconceptions of NLP, some of which describe NLP as some kind of dogmatic or esoteric belief system. This could not be further from the flexibility that is the true nature of NLP. It is a science that provides a context for discovery without the limitations of beliefs or theories.

The dogmatic, sometimes delusional, 'happy-clappy' cult of NLP is a direct result of the way in which it is marketed in many cases. The methodology seems to be more about creating a euphoric experience and a catalyst for immediate and potentially short-term change than actually imparting anything of long-term value to the individual. Some training courses even have a condition that feedback forms must be completed before the individual leaves the room at the end of the training while they are still in a euphoric state. This is not genuine feedback; it is collecting testimonials.

I nearly left the world of NLP as quickly as I found it. When I was at Master Practitioner level I was frequently using the patterns in coaching and training, practising the patterns at any given opportunity and obsessively constructing new patterns; and even with NLP consuming this much of my attention, I was reluctant to mention NLP in my marketing or in application. Although I valued what I had gained from NLP personally, and the methodology I had learnt underpinned everything I was doing, I did not want to be associated with the general perception of NLP.

I then had the good fortune to meet John Grinder and Carmen Bostic St Clair who provided me with an experience of the subject that I can congruently and wholeheartedly represent to others, and access to a community of trainers that I am happy to be associated with. Again, I thank Michael Carroll at The NLP Academy for facilitating this. Michael is instrumental in raising the standard of NLP in the UK, providing access to John, Carmen and several other amazing individuals.

If you find my approach to the subject agreeable, then I recommend for the benefit of your personal development that you avoid seminars attended by hundreds of people which are masquerading as training courses.

Also beware of trainers who market themselves with the words, "I can..." (it would be more realistic to say, "you can and I can show you how"). It is the illusion of power over another person, or the perception of a loss of control on the part of the client that contributes to much of the resistance to NLP.

I hugely enjoyed the recently published by Derren Brown entitled *Trick of the Mind* (Channel 4 Books, 2006)

Apart from a fundamental misunderstanding about NLP Modelling, Brown raises some very reasonable and legitimate questions about the patterns and techniques of NLP and provides some well-earned criticism of the NLP community.

By his account, he attended an NLP Practitioner training course with a company that trains hundreds of people at one time with little or no individual attention from the trainers – more of a seminar than a training course.

I was pleased that Brown did distinguish and exclude John Grinder from this criticism. I would recommend that anyone involved with NLP read this book. If NLP is to survive as the powerful scientific methodology conceived by Bandler and Grinder in the 1970s, these criticisms need to be acknowledged and intelligently addressed.

Lastly, as I recommend to my practitioners, experience a variety trainers for a more balanced and diverse perspective; and find an opportunity to share an experience with John Grinder and Carmen Bostic St Clair if and when you can.

To conclude this section:

- This workbook contains only the patterns of NLP that can be experienced (albeit in a limited way) through this limited type of media (a book).

- Although the patterns and techniques of NLP can be applied to anything, their implementation is made specific to make them easier to utilise in your every day life.

- The presuppositions of NLP are scattered throughout the workbook and referred to as 'big ideas'.

- If you can develop the ability to take on a new idea and act *'as if'* it is true you can better evaluate it without prejudice, and then accept or reject it based upon the results you get.

- There is dogshit attached to the shoe of NLP and it will need to be cleaned up if NLP is to take its rightful place as a legitimate methodology for scientific endeavour.

1. The Science Bit

It was Christmas Day 1980 (give or take a year). My family celebrate Christmas and we exchange gifts on Christmas morning.

My brother (who is four years my junior) and I were given an eagerly anticipated ATARI games console by our parents. We spent the day in a highly excited state about being given this completely new system to learn and play with.

After what seemed like days, in reality a couple of hours, the games console found itself attached to the television. My brother and I sat next to each other with controller in hand, poised to begin what became an epic battle with huge jagged blobs of colour that represented duelling tanks or 'dogfighting' aircraft.

As soon as we began playing it became immediately clear that there was a gulf between our levels of ability and hand-screen coordination. I beat my sibling convincingly, consistently and without reprieve.

At first, I assume, he was too busy acquainting himself with the basic operation to the game to pay much attention to the results he was getting. After some time he had established a basic competence and seemed to become more competitive.

He then began to become angered by the constant defeat. He concentrated intensely and focused on the coloured blobs of pixels moving around the screen, gritting his teeth and reacting more and more dramatically to each defeat.

Somewhere just short of despair, he suddenly stopped looking at the screen and began looking at me. He began to search desperately for some clue as to what I was doing that he was not. He had exhausted everything that he could learn from observing the results of our actions on the screen; he was now desperate to learn something else and hoping that observing me would provide some insight into what I was doing to cause the different results.

Unfortunately, he was not in a fit 'state' to observe the differences in our behaviour and was far too firmly in the grips of frustration to experiment with his own behaviour. But he had the right idea.

In observing the difference between one person's performance and another's, there is only so much we can learn from comparing the results of their actions; there is far more to be learnt from the differences in their processes and the behaviours that get those results.

It is obviously difficult to guess explicitly what someone else is doing, because we have only our existing frame of reference, but we can emulate their behaviour and experience the difference for ourselves.

33

Please note: With the exception of the author's opinion and examples, the content of the following chapter is simply an accessible paraphrase of the epistemology presented by John Grinder and Carmen Bostic St Clair in 'Whispering in the wind'.

If you wish to reference any of the ideas within the chapter please refer back to the source material.

Although the intention in writing this book is to provide practical communication skills in the context of business, the subject matter is some of the patterns and techniques of NLP. As such, it is important to pay some attention to the foundations of the NLP model.

This is not a 'textbook' on the subject of NLP, so we will address only that which you need to know at this point on your NLP journey.

I considered omitting this section completely. However, I feel that it provides a frame of reference that is vital to developing a practical understanding of some of the 'big ideas' and communication patterns featured in this book.

Epistemology studies the nature of the knowledge and presuppositions that are the foundation of a subject and their validity. A simple definition would be: **How we know what we know?**

An important characteristic of the flexibility required for real NLP modelling is that the observers do not delude themselves into thinking that the observations made are anything other than observations. The act of attempting to consciously and deductively explain the thought patterns that are going on behind what is being observed limits the experience dramatically.

A more accurate definition of epistemology is: **How we know what (we think) we know?**

There are no theories in NLP. The subject does not concern itself with why things happen. Instead it impartially observes what happens and how it happens.

Much of the activity called science sets out with a theory from which hypotheses are generated and then attempts to prove or disprove them. And guess what, that's exactly what happens. If you set out with a defined hypothesis, it will come from within the realms of your current thinking. You then set out to prove or disprove the hypothesis, and that's precisely what you get. It's startling that the aim of doing research is to discover what is supposedly known in advance.

When the outcome of a research project does not fall into this anticipated result range ('significance' is not obtained), it is generally considered a failure and therefore not published. Only studies that support what is expected are published and this serves to support the underpinning paradigm or theory.

To help me articulate this, John Grinder pointed me in the direction of Thomas Kuhn (*The Structure of Scientific Revolutions, University of Chicago Press 1970*).

Normal science is the mopping-up operations of making deductions from the current paradigm and then running experiments to verify the predicted phenomenon and refine the measurements involved, in an attempt to force nature into the preformed and relatively inflexible box that the paradigm supplies.

This activity contrasts with the revolutionary replacement of one dominant paradigm with a new one.

A *shift* in professional commitments to a shared paradigm takes place when an *anomaly* or *set of anomalies* "subverts the existing tradition of scientific practice". These shifts are what Kuhn describes as *scientific revolutions* – "the tradition-shattering complements to the tradition-bound activity of normal science".

This gives birth to a highly exciting and unstable period in the development of a discipline, like the move from Newtonian physics to relativity. When this happens, "a scientist's world is qualitatively transformed [and] quantitatively enriched by fundamental novelties of either fact or theory."

The challenge is that, to be accepted, new assumptions paradigms require the reconstruction of prior assumptions and the re-evaluation of prior facts. This is difficult, time-consuming and typically strongly resisted by the established community.

In the context of NLP, when we consider our objective of observing excellence in the behaviour of individuals, there are two flaws to the more traditional scientific approach:

Firstly, as humans our attention direction is limited when we are being deductive and focused. Anything important that we perceive as falling outside of the boundaries set by defining a hypothesis is ignored completely. We will unconsciously consider it to be irrelevant. It's not what we are looking for, so we will simply delete it from our awareness. (As per the example in the previous chapter – whilst we are looking to identify the fruit we are not considering the vegetable encyclopaedia).

Secondly, when you have a well-defined hypothesis, you will be observing from that frame of reference and you will easily gather evidence to support it. We have a tendency to distort things to fit within what we expect. (We will find the fruit that is closest to it.)

Scientists are aware of this 'confirmation bias' so they set out to disprove what they believe to be true. Their success in doing this in active observation will be entirely subject to their ability to truly let go of their beliefs and expectations. I would venture that in many cases there is little difference between distorting information to prove what you expect or believe, and distorting information to *not disprove* what you expect or believe, when the original hypothesis is held within your current 'frame of reference'.

This brings me to another interesting idea:

Have you ever noticed that, when you decide to buy a certain type of car, there suddenly seems to be an enormous number of that particular type of car on the road? It's almost like every fourth car is the same type as the one you are buying.

Last year my wife was pregnant. Whenever we went out there were pregnant women everywhere! This year my wife gave birth to a beautiful baby boy. I have no idea where all the pregnant women went, but now there are babies everywhere! Overnight all of the restaurants are suddenly displaying 'baby changing' signs – I'm sure they weren't there before, were they?

We constantly set a 'frame' around our experience that selects what we pay attention to. There is so much going on we cannot possibly take it all in. Our 'frame of reference' governs what we pay conscious attention to and what we ignore.

In modelling excellence in human behaviour, we have no idea what we are looking for – we do not know in advance how the individual is getting the results that they are getting. We could develop theories and set out to prove or disprove them, but these theories are our best guesses based on the evidence that we have consciously noticed, from our existing understanding, knowledge or awareness.

We can be fairly sure that the results Bandler and Grinder achieved in modelling Milton Erickson *(the model from whom we have the Milton Model which you will encounter in part later in this book)* simply could not have been achieved through conventional scientific modelling.

There are no theories in NLP. There are, however, presuppositions that it operates from (in this book they are the 'big ideas), and even these are flexible.

These presuppositions act as constructive or useful things to believe – believing them sets up a neurological filter that will get you excellent results in your communication and behaviour. However, if the belief becomes definite and inflexible it filters your experience in the same way as setting up a compelling and well defined hypothesis. This is why the 'as if' frame in the previous chapter is important. Beliefs are powerful filters and can be very resourceful, and can also be limiting without the ability to 'turn them off' occasionally.

Some academics have rejected NLP on the basis that it is not empirically proven. As a practitioner of NLP you are likely to be confronted by this argument so I would like to spend the next couple of pages addressing it.

When I last looked up NLP on Wikipedia it read: "In the late 80's the United States National Research Council gave NLP a negative assessment."

Despite challenge from the conventional scientific community, NLP has not gone away; in fact it continues to grow. I believe there is a need for more critical study of NLP, and many 'definitions' of NLP provided by qualified Practitioners or trainers (often with the intention of marketing) are so un-scientific that they serve to discredit the discipline altogether. Many of my own explicit definitions are barely competent.

My immediate comments on this subject would be:

There is a difference between not proven and disproved – NLP is a relatively new science and there is simply not enough serious research into the field at present.

Many initial flaws in how Bandler and Grinder first communicated NLP to the world have been 'cleaned up' by The New Code[*].

Some Master Trainers have added questionable content-based assumptions and explanations to the expanding and diversifying field of NLP.

The successful application of the patterns of NLP is subject to the ability levels of the practitioner, and these vary widely. It is a pragmatic process that makes few universal statements and cannot be sensibly analysed by statistics. It functions more like algebra; with a precise,

---

[*] John Grinder has been developing the New Code of NLP since 1988; working first with Judith DeLozier and more recently with Carmen Bostic St Clair.

hands-on observational approach, working only with specific, visible, sensory information and states equivalence only when it can be clearly observed and there is no observed exception to it at that time.

Although NLP is clearly a scientific activity, the utilisation of NLP at a level of unconscious competence is more of an art.

I would also remind you that many of the patterns of NLP are not NLP itself. NLP is a modelling science. The models are only as useful as the behaviours on which they are based. The techniques of NLP are resourceful perceptions and amazingly effective metaphors rather than an attempt to gain explicit understanding of what's going on within the individual.

By addressing NLP from a conventional scientific perspective, you may have completely missed the point. It's like using a ruler to measure temperature, or a thermometer to measure length.

Human behaviour is inexplicably subtle and sophisticated. NLP, as a process, captures more information than can be consciously collected through observation and reasoning as a detached observer; experimenting with one theory after another. Only by applying our perceptive abilities that are beyond reasoning, even beyond words, can we begin to gain some kind of awareness of what is really happening (rather than our opinion of what may be happening and what we can empirically 'prove'). By the way – does empirical proof make something right? Aren't previously empirically proven theories being superseded all the time?

I would like to relay a story that came to my attention in *Blink – The Power of Thinking Without Thinking* by Malcolm Gladwell (Penguin, 2006).

Among the many fascinating cases that Gladwell pulls together in this book are some discoveries made by the professional tennis coach Vic Braden. Braden found that, when he asked several professional players about their technique, not a single one of them was consistent in knowing what he/she was doing.

For example, almost every player in the world will tell you that they roll their wrist over the ball when they hit a forehand. Braden has digitised footage of players, frame-by-frame so that he can measure this rotation in the wrist by an eighth of a degree, and found that players almost never move their wrist at all.

In having to consciously explain the activity of hitting a forehand, the player is attempting to explain an inexplicable amount of calculations and actions that all take place in a fraction of a second. The only way to understand such an activity is to do it and make tiny, unperceivable changes to the technique in response to the results that you are getting – the path of the ball after leaving the racquet.

The tennis players' conscious understanding of what they are doing is not what is really happening. I always thought that I rolled my wrist – I guess it's a metaphoric description of what it feels like when the wrist is kept straight rather than a description of what is really happening.

Here's another way of looking at it.

How can you empirically prove what makes one painting beautiful and another very similar painting average? *(Accepting that this is a value judgement and therefore unquantifiable – one person's music is another person's noise)*

There are plenty of individual factors that you could theorise about – thickness and weight of brush strokes, use of contrasting colour, proportions of the subject matter – and you are loosing sight of the inexplicable quality of the painting.

Even if these details that you theorise about are the contributory factors to a great painting, understanding them will not make you a great artist.

Let's look at a fresh example to illustrate the NLP approach to modelling.

Let's imagine that you have identified an individual who is a model of excellence; someone who gets amazing results and we mere mortals have no idea how they are doing it. Let's add in the fact that these abilities have not been witnessed before. Rather than something they have learned to a very proficient level, they are the creator of this behaviour; it's an innate and inexplicable ability; nobody else can do this and get the same results. A good example would be Milton Erickson or a model that Dr John Grinder has recently been working with – Monty Roberts 'the horse whisperer'.

We have two options in gaining insight into this:

1. We can observe the model and guess what about their behaviour may have a cause/effect relationship with the observable results we are seeing. We can then conduct further observation and set up experiments in an attempt to prove statistically whether that specific behaviour is significant or not. (In creating laboratory experiments we may be removing some of the conditions that are significant to the result).

This is a guessing game. We are guessing what they might be doing and then setting out to discover if we were right. We can only hypothesize from our own tacit knowledge and current frame of reference, and if we have no idea what the model is doing it could take a lot of guesses. Even if we do discover a significant pattern, how do we know when we have captured all of the patterns that contribute to the results? When are we finished with this process, when do we stop?

2. We can physically model the subject through the replication of micro muscle movement, with no attempt to consciously comprehend, until we can emulate their behaviour to such a degree that we can achieve the same results as the model in the same time or less. When we can do this it's safe to assume that we have captured the entire model – all of the behaviours that are significant to the results.

Notice at this point we still have no idea what the individual is doing, yet we can do it, so we have captured all of the patterns and we can begin to investigate by isolating and removing one pattern at a time. If the removal of an isolated pattern adversely affects the results then it is significant. It is part of the effective behaviour and we can begin to code it. If removal of an isolated behaviour has no effect, that behaviour is an idiosyncratic behaviour of the individual and not related to the modelled activity.

When studying other sciences like physics for example, we have no other option but to use option 1. We cannot actually observe sub-atomic particles and must 'assume' their existence in order to create a hypothesis that we can then test with practical experimentation. We tend to create metaphors of our observable physical world and apply them to that which we cannot observe – the model that springs to mind is ping-pong balls in a glass jar used to demonstrate how a gas behaves under pressure – decrease the volume of the glass jar and the ping pong balls have less space between them, so they collide with each other and the sides of the jar more frequently. Obviously gas atoms do not really look or behave like ping pong balls. It's just a metaphor for us to work with the unobservable.

Once a metaphoric model like this is created, experiments can be conducted in reality to see if the results in reality are as the model would predict.

If this is proven the model is proven to be useful – but not proven to be true. We can never really know the truth because it is not possible to observe – it can only really be considered a useful model.

In addition, we cannot 'be' an alpha particle and then ask what made us leave the nucleus of an atom. Silly suggestion I know, but think about it for a minute: When addressing human behaviour, surely we are able to utilise our own human system to create an accurate frame of reference rather than the 'best guesses' of a detached observer.

I regularly practise karate and occasionally teach. If I were teaching a pattern of movement, I would do it and encourage the students to copy. I may also use metaphor like, "Imagine you have no shoulder" (like the rolling the wrist example) to communicate the intention of the movement and draw the student's attention inside their body.

Imagine if I were to just talk about the principle of karate, maybe draw a couple of diagrams and explain why it works without demonstration or practice. The students may be able to talk about karate and believe they understood exactly what it is; but how useful would this knowledge be without any awareness of application?

I would like to make it clear that my intention is not to criticise psychology or any other fields of human study that are based in conventional scientific analysis (I value psychology, some of my colleagues that I collaborate with are psychologists and I reference several psychologists in this book). I am simply differentiating them from NLP as they operate in a fundamentally different way.

Psychology is to statistics as NLP is to algebra.

Assessing NLP by the measures applied to other sciences is interesting and provides valuable criticism of the NLP models, but it's assessing NLP with the very reasoning that the subject set out to avoid from conception.

Many other fields concern themselves with identifying what is 'normal'. What people 'generally' do, (proven by what is considered to be an acceptable statistical bias) and to understand 'why' this is the case. NLP is an exploration into what is exceptional, and sets out to code the process of the exceptional behaviour. In the pursuit of excellence we can learn little form the tendencies of the masses (although the identification of what is normal helps us to identify what is exceptional).

By the way; NLP is often considered un-scientific or un-academic. This is ridiculous to me; the process-based NLP methodology is cleaner than other content-based scientific methods. Also NLP takes its theoretical underpinnings from many intellectual giants including Noam Chomsky, Gregory Bateson and Milton Erickson and features presuppositions from gestalt psychology, family systems therapy, Ericksonian hypnotic-medical communication, general-semantics, cybernetics, information systems, transformational grammar, cognitive-behavioural psychology, and Batesonian anthropology.

On our continued journey of discovery into human behaviour there is need for both scientific theory and process, and a more unconscious assimilation of behavioural information that is consciously inexplicable at the level of understanding we are currently operating from.

I recently enjoyed reading *Screw It Let's Do It* by Richard Branson (Virgin Books). It struck me that, Richard Branson is constantly presented with well researched, high quality statistics and business critical information about his airline from the many capable people who run it. And yet he frequently boards his own aircraft and talks to the passengers in person to collect valuable feedback. He is in the business of running an airline, not interpreting statistics. I'm in the business of working with people.

I choose to have a bit of a problem with some applications of statistics in human studies – whilst useful for identifying trends in a population, they are a bit of an unacceptable imposition when their findings are applied back against the individual with any degree of **certainty**.

To illustrate this I would invite you firstly to consider that the obvious fact that the wider we 'cast the net' to collect sample data the less relevant and therefore reliable it is. For example: The world population is currently about 6.7 billion people. More than 1.2 billion of them are Chinese. That means nearly 20% of the world population are Chinese (I have rounded up a couple of percent for simplicity). If we selected a member of the world population at random they have a 1/5 chance of being Chinese. If we apply this statistic to a smaller geography than 'the world' the statistic is no longer true: In the UK less than 1/5 people will be Chinese, and in China it will be more than 1/5.

This is just as true when we take data from multiple subjects, no matter how refined the sample data, and apply it to the individual – If I were that individual I would protest that the data can't be very precise in my case because, whoever the sample subjects were they weren't all me.

And it's only accurate in terms of probability and is completely useless in confronting a specific individual or member of the reference group.

For example; I work in a geographical area where there is 3% unemployment. Does that mean I have a 3/100 chance of being unemployed?

In the world of statistics; yes – if you happen to pick me at random from that demographic that is the probability that I'm unemployed.

In the real world; No – some individuals will be more likely to be unemployed and others less because of their **individual abilities, history and experience.**

I have no idea if you are familiar with the Myers Briggs Type Indicator (MBTI). Mother and daughter Myers & Briggs created a behavioural psychometric that can be a great first step on the road to self-awareness. You may have already encountered this psychometric, as it is used by many organisations.*

First published in 1942, the MBTI test added a further dimension to Carl Jung's 'Psychological Types'. An additional personality dimension, a theory of Myers, governed how the functions of Jung's types work together and enabled the creation of 16 personality profiles. The result, although a great example of the human tendency to carve things up and define them as one thing or another, can be a useful tool when applied to a population because it is very *likely* to be true and provides an empowering language for team interaction.

The first three dimensions were discovered as 'archetypes' by Carl Jung. He was fascinated by, and devoted his life to exploring the mysterious depths of the human unconscious. He did not feel that experimental natural science was the best means to understand the human soul. Rather than building upon what he learnt from Freud, Jung was able to free himself from the conditioning of his education.

For him, an investigation of the world of dream, myth, and soul represented the most promising road to deeper understanding. He would frequently enter states of unconsciousness to reconcile his consciousness

---

* MBTI is a great practical psychometric for understanding attention directions and communication styles of individuals on a surface level within a particular context provided it is utilised as an indication of tendencies rather than a factual, universally correct, limiting, 'pigeon holing' exercise used to define people; I wince when I hear something like, "I'm useless at that because I'm an 'INFP'". It's like a self-aware limitation, not only has the individual created or increased their difficulty in performing a particular activity; they have now made it a permanent condition. Bear in mind from a behavioural point of view that even the most inflexible of people behave differently from one context to another.

with this broader world, and learn its symbolic language.

In his practice, he would play with children's toys on the floor between sessions to enter a 'state' of creative and flexible thought, to remove conditioned limitations and re-capture the resources of flexible thought and learning we all have as children.

The utilisation of resourceful, high performance and unconscious states is generally a characteristic of 'genius' and fundamental to NLP.

As well as the utilisation of resourceful states, there is a degree of art involved in NLP modelling and also in utilising the patterns of NLP. The terminology used does not fit into the usual definitions used by psychological or behavioural sciences. Bandler & Grinder decided to deliberately use different terminology to differentiate NLP from traditional sciences in a similar field.

In this section, rather than providing some 'text book' style content for you to 'learn', I would like to build a model of how we interact with the world using your experiences and making you aware of your internal processes. Just ask yourself, instinctively; is it true, can you relate to it? Does this provide an agreeable and useful metaphor to communicate your experience of your world?

How real is real?

How do you know what you are seeing right now is real? If you closed your eyes and imagined a picture, the same neurons would be firing in you brain as would be firing if you were actually seeing the picture.

As far a science can tell, there is no difference in your brain between something you are imagining and something you are 'seeing'. How do you know what you are really seeing?

When you see something, you are seeing your representation of it, not the thing itself. You are beginning creating a map of the territory, this map is not printed on paper; it is made up of the information from your five senses.

How do you know that the picture you have of something you are looking at is identical to the person standing next to you? You cannot possibly know that. It's one of the classic questions of philosophy, when you and another person see a colour that you agree is green, how do you know you are seeing the same colour?

If you have not already, I would urge you to watch the first film in

The Matrix Trilogy. It presents a fascinating and 'mind-bending' idea.

To provide a brief synopsis; the humans in the film do not live in the physical world they think they do. Instead they are living in 'pods' connected to a giant computer. This computer is plugged into their nervous system and feeds them with an artificial world, and all of the pictures, sounds, feelings, smells and tastes that accompany their experiences in that artificial world.

The real 'mind-bender' is, if this were true, we would have no way of knowing. All we have to create our 'realities' is our five senses, and if we are able to imagine sensations in all of those senses, how real is real? How do you know? Let's look at this in more detail...

The experience that we do receive through our five senses is fairly limited. For example, the retina of our eye is unable to register frequencies of light that are outside of our visual spectrum. We know that images exist in the bandwidth of infra-red or ultra-violet (we have developed optical equipment that can show us) and they are outside of the bandwidth of our human sensory apparatus.

To us a dog whistle is silent to the human ear, yet we know that it is producing a sound because we can observe the dog reacting to it, or monitor it with listening equipment.

Can you feel still air against your skin? Are you aware of things that 'don't really smell or taste of anything'?

So before we go on to describe a model of how (we think) we process the world around us, can we first accept that, outside of the realms of our limited five senses, we have no idea what's really going on out there?

We have no way of observing everything that is going on outside of us. It's not accessible to us through our limited senses.

In New Code terminology the restricted information that is able to be sensed by our human sensory apparatus is labelled F^1.

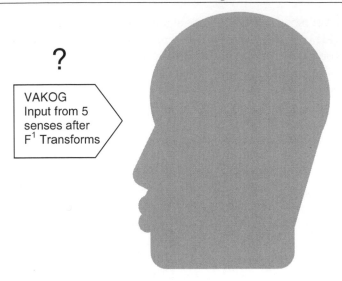

All we can experience is FA

So, by the time whatever's going on out there has been cut down by the limited bandwidth of our sensory apparatus, that information is then transformed in ways that we cannot possibly be aware of.

For example the F^1 visual representation consists of two separate images, one from each eye, yet our first access experience is of one three-dimensional image.

Our auditory information comes from two ears. Sound waves approaching us from the left will strike the ear drum of our left ear earlier and with more volume than the right. Yet our experience is of one sound and a spatial awareness of the origin of the sound.

These neurological transforms clearly alter the original information to create a manageable representation, and in reality it is impossible for us to be certain of that process.

We have no way of experiencing anything before these neurological transforms have happened.

The representation we are provided with after these neurological transforms is labelled FA – First Access.

It is our immediate experience of the world. It's just the sensory information – we have yet to apply any meaning to it. It is the raw data before we have made any judgements about that information.

So for example, if we see a door, the visual information of the door (colours, shades and lines) has reached our mind, but we have not done the logical typing, naming function of deciding it's a door. Our instinctive judgements or filters of language have not been applied yet.

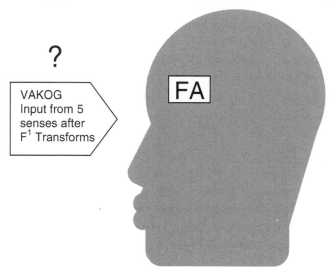

V = Visual (Pictures)
A = Auditory (Sounds)
K = Kinaesthetic (Feelings)
O = Olfactory (Smells)
G = Gustatory (Tastes)

This does not make sense......yet

This first access experience is pure experience, not constrained by the comparative, judgemental and limiting qualities of language.

You are being flooded with information through your five senses that has no 'meaning' – it's simply a pure experience.

You now begin to 'make sense' of what you are receiving from your senses. This is an instinctive process. You apply linguistic transforms – 'filters' that you have acquired mainly through past experiences.

So, if you can imagine receiving information before any instinctive thought processes have been applied, the kind of judgements we make or 'filters' we apply would be something like the following example:

Let's say, to use the same example as earlier, we look and see a door. As soon as we have received the visual information we begin instinctively classifying what we are seeing into the 'set' of things called 'doors'.

By the way, it's interesting to notice that nouns are not specific descriptions – they are the name of a collection or 'set' of items. A door does not have a specific size or shape, and it is not made from a specific material – some are wood, some are glass; some pivot on hinges, others slide. So the noun does not describe the item, it describes the set – providing the often unspecified boundary conditions or parameters that allow us to classify it. The process of identifying an item as a door will limit the experience of a particular door – you will pay little attention to it as an experience – you have already grouped it with past experiences of doors.

The process of defining a noun is complicated enough; imagine what processes are involved in defining something less tangible.

So the information arrives from our senses, judgements are made about the information by applying linguistic transforms, the results of which is your 'map of the world'. In defining and naming these things within this map you will have imposed your filters (experience, values, beliefs, perceptions, attention directions, attitudes and other products of your language) upon it.

The above paragraph is a metaphor to provide a frame of reference to reason with what we can observe ourselves doing. Does everyone use the same 'filters'? Are they applied to experience in a certain order? Are they arranged in a hierarchy? Who knows? An individual thought may contain several of these processes, they happen too quickly for us to isolate and observe, and they may be different for different people.

Applying the linguistic transforms of the naming function creates the rules and boundaries of our 'model of the world' and constricts our interpretation of the world even further. We now have even less idea of what's really going on out there.

The VAKOG information of the FA experience is further reduced by our F^2 linguistic transforms – segmented and classified by the imposition of filters and words.

Here's a practical example of the F^2 linguistic transforms imposed upon your experience of the world:

Look at the chequered panel below and observe square A and square B. Would you say that one of them is darker/lighter than the other?

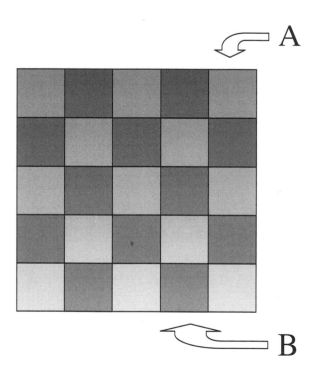

How about now?

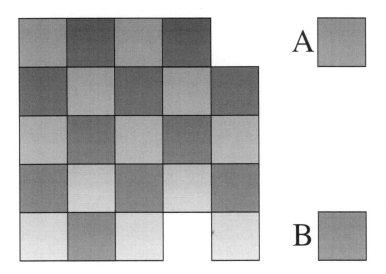

They are actually the same square.

This is an example of the comparative, labeling F^2 linguistic transforms imposing themselves upon our FA experience of the world.

As we look at the grid, our F^2 linguistic transforms 'make sense' of it by comparing the squares to the squares around them and categorizing the squares into one of two sets; light squares or dark squares.

A is classified as a light square; B is classified as a dark square.

This is often described as an optical illusion, but there is nothing optical about it. In terms of the light falling on the retina and stimulating the optic nerve A and B are the same.

It is the comparative evaluation and classification of A and B that corrupts our FA experience.

I think for this imposition as a two-way street as our interpretation of our FA experience creates the rules and boundaries of the 'map'.

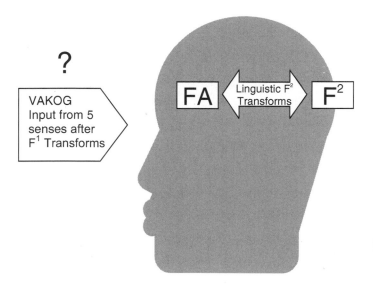

This F^2 internal representation of what's going on provides us with a frame of reference from which we behave and communicate.

Our F^2 representations or our 'map of the world' is reflected in our behaviour (language and physiology or 'body language').

This is probably a good point to take a moment to consider how limited your conscious representation of an experience really is. How many details can you list about a past experience before you run out? How many details are missing? Think of a past conversation. Do you remember every little facial expression; every inflection in voice tone; every gesture? Sure you may have vivid pictures and sound bites, and generally what you remember is a perception of the interaction with more attention to certain bits while others are completely forgotten.

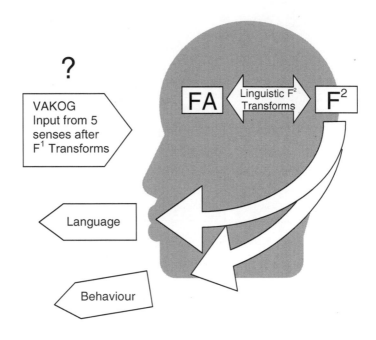

It instinctively feels to me that, if our VAKOG information is the operating system of our mind, language is the software of our conscious thought. Would you agree?

Because of the applied nature of this workbook, and its selective focus upon just some patterns and techniques, I considered completely ignoring the epistemology. However, after beginning to write, it became very clear that I was unable to communicate NLP effectively without addressing The New Code Epistemology.

It effectively communicates some ideas that will be utilised throughout the book, and is the clearest way to make the important distinction between our experience of the world and what we think is our experience of the world (what we take from it and normally accept without question).

Which brings me to a very important 'Big Idea':

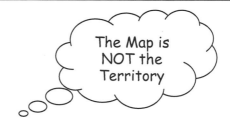

Alfred Korzybski wrote the book *Science and Sanity – An introduction to non-Aristotelean systems and general semantics* in 1933 as the old science that regarded physical objects and phenomena as unchangeable, finite constructs that could be studied in isolation began to fall apart (thanks in part to relativity theory and quantum physics). Things were found to be much more interdependent and fluid than earlier assumed.

General Semantics provides a system of studying man's relation to his world and many people regard the single most important statement to be: The Map is not the Territory.

When you look at a location on a map, even a really detailed one containing a huge amount of information, it is very different to actually being at that location.

The map is a representation of the real world – the territory.

When you read a detailed description of an item of food on a menu, you may even begin to salivate and imagine tastes or textures; and this is still different to the actual experience of eating the food when you encounter it. The description of the food is not the food. Looking at a picture of the Grand Canyon, or hearing someone describe it, is very different to standing on the edge of it.

The representation of the world we operate from is not the real world – it's just our perception of it. It's what's left after we have collected it through our senses, after the neurological transforms, and then applied the judgements of our linguistic transforms.

So, when we communicate, we do not communicate reality, because we have filtered the reality with our neurological transforms; and we cannot even communicate our FA experience, because to convert it to language we have filtered it with the judgements made by our linguistic transforms.

We communicate from our 'map'; and we all have a different 'map'. We all live in our own individual worlds that are a result of our filters or transforms.

Because we have different memories, experiences, values, beliefs, perceptions, decisions about ourselves, attention directions and attitudes, all of which may be applied to our FA experience to begin to create an individual definition of the stimulus we are being provided with – we live in different worlds.

You may have had the experience in the past, when communicating on a surface level, of saying to someone, "I know exactly where you are coming from – I see what you are saying."

I suggest that you think about this for a moment. Granted, I'm sure that there is a good level of shared ideas and agreement – but to know exactly? Is this really possible, to share the same idea in every detail?

When someone describes something to you, you use your imagination or memory to make sense of what they are describing. So the representation you have in your mind is the product of your imagination or memory, not exactly what the speaker has in their mind. For example; when someone describes their state as 'excited' you have no idea what that excitement feels like to them – you can use your meaning of excited, or how excited feels to you in a similar context, and it will probably be different to their 'excited'.

When someone provides you with some words, their 'map' you still have no idea about their 'territory'.

Another empowering thing to be aware of is that most of our problems exist in our 'map' and not 'the territory'. If there is something that has been bothering you recently, ask yourself; how is it a problem for you at this exact moment in time as you read this page and continue to breathe? The chances are, unless you are in immediate danger, your problems are comparisons or judgements about something in the past you are dwelling on or something in an imagined future that has not happened.

Getting yourself in a 'state'

You are no doubt familiar with the expression 'state of mind'. Perhaps you have heard someone say, "I'm in a state".

An introductory working definition of 'state' would be 'how you feel about the situation you are in'. (In reality, we are often unaware of our own state because we are 'in it', until we learn a way of gaining perspective).[*]

For the purpose of this workbook, you need only have an awareness of what 'state' is, what are the effects of state and how state can be affected.

We will not be working directly with state because of the limited nature of this media. However, using the thought processes, patterns and techniques within this book you are likely to notice changes to your state in future scenarios.

Allow me to illustrate what I mean by state:

Firstly, let's consider a scenario for which you will be able to create a certain type of internal representation:

You are sitting in an office reviewing something that has gone wrong. I don't know if it would be easier for you to imagine a problem with financials, logistics, quality, communication or something else. You are the person 'responsible' for whatever it is that's gone wrong and you are working with someone who has voiced their disappointment with the actions you chose.

How would you be feeling? (What 'state' would you be in?)

Also notice how you would be sitting. What would your voice tone be like? Notice how you would be breathing or what your facial expression would be.

Now let's consider a similar scenario for which you will have a different type of internal representation:

You are in the same office with the same person. This time they are reviewing your performance and they are delighted with what they are seeing. They are looking to promote you and, in the meantime, will be giving you a substantial pay rise. As they are telling you this with a smile on their face and inviting your comments:

How would you be feeling? (What 'state' would you be in?)

Also notice how you would be sitting. What would your voice tone be like? Notice how you would be breathing or what your facial expression would be.

---

[*] Working with state is extremely important. I'm heavily influenced by Grinder and Bostic, and one of their current assertions is that 'it's all about state'. Without the utilisation of high performance states real NLP modelling cannot be achieved, without calibrating on state we have no awareness of what's going on in our world or that of another person, all NLP change techniques can be made with awareness of state and free of content and there is an improved effectiveness and ecology in doing so.

Same office; different F^2 representation of what's going on, and therefore a different 'state' and different behaviour.

So we can agree that a change in your internal representation (what you think about the situation) changes your 'state'.

We can also notice that a change in your state will change you physiology & behaviour (body language, breathing, voice tone, choice of words etc.) So a communication model would look something like this:

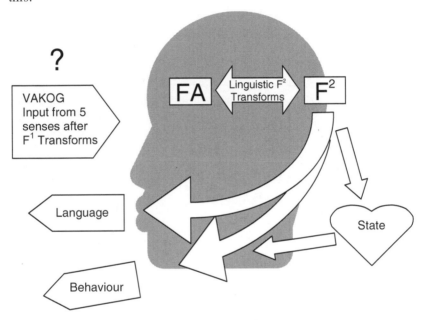

A change at F^2 (your internal representation of what's going on like a positive or negative meeting) will change your state (how you feel about it).

A change of state will change how you behave (body language, voice tone, breathing, facial expressions etc.)

Now here's where it gets a bit less obvious and even more interesting:

Instinctively, you may think that our state is reflected in our behaviour; almost like it's a sequential, 'cause→effect' relationship.

You may think something like, "I get in a particular state and then I behave in a particular way." It's almost like the behaviour reflects what's going on inside.

Well, it's a bit more than that. The change can be effected both ways.

We have discovered that if your state changes, your body language changes. It works both ways.

If you change your body language you will change your state.

If you are having a 'wet Wednesday afternoon' feeling with a 'slumped' body language, and you lift your head, throw your shoulders back, breath deeply and smile, the negative feeling will be gone.

The 'wet Wednesday afternoon' state cannot exist when you have positive physiology.

Try it – slouch in your chair, drop your head and allow yourself to think of a situation when you feel a bit unmotivated.

Now sit up, lift your head, take long deep breaths and allow a smile to creep in, and notice how differently you feel, even when the situation that you are thinking of is the same both times.

Changing physiology changes how you feel about a situation; which brings us to another 'Big Idea':

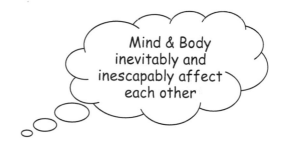

Mind & Body
inevitably and
inescapably affect
each other

It is damaging to assume that the mind and body are separate. Rather than mind and body, it would be a bit better to refer to the relationship as mind-body, and better still to give up on these segmented definitions all together. It is one system; no part functions independently of another.

As we have seen in the previous section, the mind affects what's going on with the body and the body affects what's going on with the mind. It would be even more accurate to say that it is happening simultaneously.

If you would like to evaluate this for yourself, please play along with the following experiment:

1. Stand with your feet apart (about the width of your shoulders), extend your right arm in front of you and rotate to your right as far is as comfortable without moving your feet. Look along your arm to notice how far you have rotated.

2. Keeping your arm in front of you, close your eyes and, without moving, imagine in detail doing the same movement five times – notice all the muscle groups that are involved in the movement.

3. Now do the first movement again and notice how far you are able to rotate this time.

The placebo effect is another good example of how a change in thought process or belief (therefore a change to F^2) causes physiological change.

For years doctors have experimented by giving one patient a placebo (an inert sugar tablet) and another patient active medicine to see if the effect of the drug occurs because of the effect of chemicals present in the drug or because the patient believes they have received medicine.

Many experiments have shown a reduction in symptoms when a placebo was used, some have shown exceptional results with the placebo outperforming the actual drug.

This is a fantastic example of the mind-body system. A change in belief will result in a physical change.

It's the same with the relationship between state and your F^2 internal representation.

Obviously, the F^2 representation provides the information that provokes the state. Change the state and you will change the F^2 representation.

So the model now looks like this:

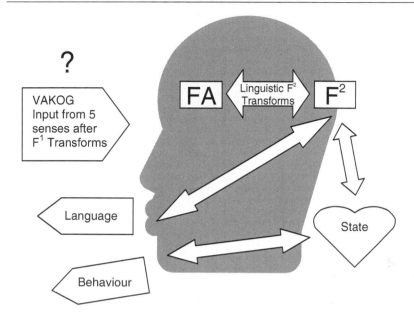

The purpose of the arrows is simply to illustrate that your F^2 internal representation, your state, and your behaviour are linked in such a way that a change in any one of them will change the other two.

This does not suggest any kind of organisation, sequence or structure of these processes. It's simply a model that suggests the effects of a change at F^2, physiology or state.

Again, I urge you to test this:

Think of a situation:

1. Change your body language, notice how you feel differently about it (state), and it then changes your perception of it (F^2).

2. Add in a new positive belief, decision or attitude (change a filter to change the F^2 representation). Notice how you feel differently about it (state). Notice how your physiology has changed (behaviour).

3. Change how you feel, imagine a different feeling in that situation, the kind of feeling that you get in a very positive situation (change state). Notice how you physiology changes (behaviour), notice how you can now perceive the situation differently.

I'm not sure if, at this stage, you will have the flexibility to conduct the experiment above. Also, this exercise is one that can be difficult to experience from reading a book. If you achieved a conclusive and convincing result; well done, you will be good at this NLP stuff.[*]

If physiology, state and our F^2 'map' of the world are linked, what does this mean? It means that you can be 'Response – Able'.

This 'Big Idea' is that you can choose your response to any stimulus.

NLP offers Neuro-Linguistic processes for taking control of our thought processes.

I would like to share this quote from Richard Bandler (1985):

"I want you to find out how you can learn to change your own experience, and get some control over what happens in your brain. Most people are prisoners of their own brains. It is as if they are chained to the last seat of the bus and someone else is driving. I want you to learn how to drive your own bus. If you don't give your brain a little direction, either it will just run randomly on its own or other people will find ways to run it for you – and they may not always have your best interests in mind. Even if they do they may get it wrong."

The one outcome that I would recommend you set for your NLP journey is to enter the driving seat of your bus.

Let go of your knee-jerk reactions that do you no favours. Put a gap between stimulus and response that provides you with choice about how to respond.

Here's an interesting way of looking at it: One choice is no choice;

---

[*] It is because of this difficulty in simultaneously reading and becoming aware of your inner processes that I have omitted much of the NLP model from this workbook. It is my personal belief, at this time, that the best way to be introduced to some of these concepts is in an experiential format – come along on a training course so that you can experience these powerful models working to full effect.

two choices is a dilemma; only with three or more options do you really have a choice.

In my experience a problem is only a problem because we only have one way of dealing with it, and that way does not work. Rather than recognise that we are not getting the result we want and changing our behaviour, we run the same unhelpful strategy of behaviour over and over again, becoming increasingly frustrated by the results we are getting. If we are inflexible about the outcome, this frustration is multiplied.

It is through the presuppositions of NLP, the 'Big Ideas' punctuated throughout this workbook that you can begin to make changes to your internal representations,

You can create more choice and free yourself from your current knee-jerk responses if you have more flexibility of how you perceive the stimulus.

The 'Big Ideas' can provide this flexibility of thought, thus providing choice over how you respond to a stimulus.

As with the earlier section on 'Cause or Effect', ask yourself who is in charge really? You may argue that you are controlled, influenced or disempowered by others – but that is not really possible. You can only do these things to yourself by putting yourself in that position.

So ask yourself – who's driving the bus?

When you take the steering wheel, you can begin to develop even more flexibility. You may need to leave the bus completely in order to check the tyres or the lights. You may even choose to take the train. When you recognise that you have response-ability, that you can choose your response to any stimulus, you can free yourself from the world of 'rules' and restrictions that you have created for yourself.

Summary

- NLP is fundamentally different to other fields of human study.

- Our experience of the world is restricted by the limitations of our senses and the boundaries created by our comparative and classifying, linguistic thought processes (our map).

- Our limited representation of the world is not the world – the map is not the territory.

- Neurology and physiology are the same system.

- We can change our state by changing either our internal representation or our physiology.

- We have the ability to choose our response to any stimulus.

2. Making a Connection

How are you getting on?

One of the skills that makes the patterns and techniques of NLP effective or even possible is the ability to create a feeling of rapport with another person extremely quickly; and maintain it.

This is extremely important. You will need to develop this ability to become an NLP Practitioner. You will need to develop the awareness and behavioural flexibility to change your language and behaviour to create an unconscious connection, an agreeable atmosphere around any interaction.

Have you ever heard the expression, "We seem to have got off on the wrong foot."? If so you may have said, "Can we start again?" You never have a second chance to create a first impression. It is possible to change people's perceptions later, and it's easier if you don't need to.

Have you ever had the experience of talking to someone for the first time and feeling that you have made a connection with them straight away; something just 'clicks', they look like the kind of person you can 'get on with', you seem to see things the same way and find them easy to understand.

Maybe it's something you can see in them, perhaps it's what they say, often you just get a feeling about someone or sometimes they think the same way as you do.

Perhaps you can think of a specific person that you 'got on with' immediately, as soon as you met them for the first time?

Have you ever wondered what is happening in this interaction? What makes them 'your kind of person?' How do you know?

It's more of a sense of something rather than anything you could specifically point out. What are you sensing? What would you say that you have noticed about them?

It's an unconscious process; you are not explicitly aware of what it is that will give you that feeling of connection; you cannot see or hear any obvious things that would lead to such a decision.

The same thing happens in reverse; have you ever had a conversation in which you are agreeing with the other person, and you somehow do not have the feeling of agreement? The 'connection' is not there.

So here's an idea: What if some people do something in their language and behaviour that you find agreeable?

You are not aware of this process, it's not something that you have consciously decided, so it would be reasonable to assume that something is going on under the surface.

Why else would you get on with some people more easily than others? What if there are subtle differences in the way they speak and behave that seems to provide clarity to the communication, you can really hear what they are saying, see their point of view and begin to feel the connection through understanding? What would those subtle differences be? How would they happen? How do you notice them without noticing them?

As you go on to discover some answers to these questions and more, I would expect you to find one consistent factor.

In this chapter we will be going on to identify some of the behaviours you can choose that will create unconscious rapport.

In order to do this we will be operating from one simple principle:

People like alike people.

It's no great secret that people like people who are like themselves. How many times do you hear the words 'we had nothing in common' as a reason for the ending of some kind of relationship?

And we all know how good it feels to be with people who share opinions, values, experiences and personal history.

Have you ever had the experience of meeting a new person that attended the same school as you, or comes from the same town; the 'small world' experience? Notice how warm you are to those people compared with a personal stranger that does not share a similar history.

The same principle applies on an unconscious level; we are drawn to people who behave in a similar way to ourselves.

What if you can develop the knowledge and flexibility to subtly change your own behaviour in a way that will be agreeable to any other individual?

This ability to create unconscious rapport with anyone is a prerequisite for the patterns and techniques of NLP.

My kind of people...

We are beginning this section with the assumption that some people exhibit behaviours that are 'alike', and we like people who are like us.

Our behaviour is a representation of the way we are thinking at the time. Everything from our choice of words and tone of voice to body language is driven by what is going on inside.

Imagine if some people used their thoughts in a similar way to us – their experience of the world would be quite similar to our own. The way they process the world will be reflected in their behaviour, so their behaviour would be similar in some way to our own. Is it possible that we are drawn to these people who 'do things' the same way we do?

I would like to share with you an abridged version of a story from *Whispering in The Wind* (Bostic/Grinder 2001) in which John Grinder relays how he and Richard Bandler (the co-creators of NLP) came to discover the patterns that are the subject of this section:

John and Richard had completed The Structure of Magic, volume 1, with the Meta model and were in the car on the way to begin a new group one evening when Richard asked John to stop at a store so that he could buy some cigarettes.

Richard stepped back into the car, laughing. John asked Richard what was so funny and he said (more or less), "You know, John, people say the weirdest things; the woman I was talking to at the counter said, 'I see what you are saying'," *and relapsed into convulsive laughter.*

John wondered what it was that made the statement so funny to Richard, and after several moments asked him, "Does the statement, 'I feel that what you are saying is unclear' strike you as funny as well?"

Richard and John then began presenting one another with example after example of the 'same' pattern without any knowledge of what the pattern was. This playful flexibility in intuitively tracking a pattern, the explication of which was some distance in the future is a reflection of the flexibility of the co-creators at the time they created NLP.

They continued generating examples of the pattern and, as they approached Santa Cruz, John stopped at a general store and purchased a sheaf of coloured paper, green, red and yellow. When they got to the place where the group was meeting (a private home), they began by inviting each of the members of the group to stand and introduce themselves.

As each member of the group finished their short self-introduction, either Richard or John would reach down, touch one of the three colours of paper and if the other one nodded, the one touching the paper would tear off a piece and present it meaningfully to the participant without explanation.

The Authors of Whispering in the Wind (Bostic and Grinder) offer several examples of typical presentations by participants to give the reader a taste of the process.

Participant 1: *Well, good evening. My name is Linda and I feel really excited about being here with all of you. I'm kinda tingly and a little nervous. My hope is to really get in touch with myself and... Participant 1 receives a yellow piece of paper.*

Participant 2: *Wow! I'm looking around the group and I see a lot of shining faces. I'm George. The picture I'm getting is real focused. What I want to take a look at is my relationship with my girlfriend and how I can help make our future even brighter... Participant 2 receives a red piece of paper.*

Participant 3: *I'm Paul, I've heard a lot of groovy stuff about these two guys here, Richard and John. Sounds to me like we gonna have a really cool time together. I was saying to myself that maybe here is a place – in other words, here is a group – where I can really tune into what's happening inside of me... Participant 3 receives a green piece of paper*

After each of the members of the group had spoken and received their piece of coloured paper, Richard and John gave them instructions to introduce themselves to other members of the group. For the first 10 minutes, they were to spend time conversing only with people who had the same colour piece of paper that they had. After 10 minutes, they were to communicate only with people who had pieces of paper of another colour. The difference between the first and second 10 minute periods was astonishing:

During the first 10 minutes which was the matching condition, there was a high volume of sound in the room, peals of laughter, animated movements and eager and receptive postures as the participants connected... all spontaneous indicators of a group of well connected people.

The second 10 minutes, the mismatching condition, couldn't have been more contrasting – low volume, fragments of conversation, periods of silence, wooden postures etc.

John writes, "As Richard and I observed the unmistakable difference between the two sessions in the same group, we realized that we were tracking a very powerful pattern."

What do we do that makes our behaviour similar in some ways to some other people, and makes it easier to 'connect' with them?

We know from the previous chapter on epistemology that there are five senses that we use to process the world around us (VAKOG).

The amount of information we receive through these senses is enormous. We are unable to 'pay attention' to all of it at once. Our consciousness pays attention to whatever we think is most appropriate at the time.

For example; you were not aware of the temperature around you until I mentioned it, or how bright/dark it is at the moment.

It's interesting to note that, if the light and temperature were to suddenly change you would be immediately consciously aware, so you are unconsciously monitoring the light and temperature at all times to the extent that you will detect any change in the light and temperature that is above threshold value.

At all times we are 'filtering' our sensory information to create an internal representation of what's going on. This internal representation will be slightly biased, 'paying attention to' some things more than others.

At any given point in time, you will be paying attention to some things more than others, and some things that are going on have been deleted from your awareness until you need to be aware of them or you are made aware of them.

We are creating or replaying internal representations at all times. Our sensory experience of the world around us, our perception of what's going on, is only the information that makes it through our various 'filters' to create an internal representation. You have an internal representation of what's going on right now.

Your current internal representation of the world will be made up of Visual, Auditory Kinaesthetic Olfactory and Gustatory (VAKOG) information, and the reasoning/comparison/classification you are applying to it.

In creating your internal representation, you will be 'favouring' some of the senses or 'representation systems' more than others. For example, you may be paying more attention to what you can see rather than what you are hearing.

The idea is that favouring one representation system will be reflected in your behaviour.

People who tend to favour the same representation system as you will behave in a similar way to you. As illustrated by John and Richard's experiment, when you encounter people who have these similar behaviours you are likely to see eye-to-eye with them, speak the same language, get a feeling of connection and know what they mean.

I know you're wondering what these similarities and differences are. We will become explicit about these behaviours later. First however, I would like you to benefit from gathering some sensory evidence of people using these different representation systems.

What are you looking for?

One of the patterns unique to NLP (as it was discovered by Bandler & Grinder) is the utilisation of eye accessing patterns. When people do a certain type of function, they look in a certain place.

You may well have heard of this. When I meet new people and tell them that I am a trainer of NLP they occasionally say, "Don't look at him. He can read your eyes."

I find this and other such mildly paranoid behaviour entertaining. Certainly it is true that, by reading the patterns of eye movement, I can see how people are thinking. I have no idea what they are thinking.

I may be able to see that someone is making a picture in their mind; I have no idea what the picture is.

I can see if they have accessed a feeling but the eye pattern alone does not tell me what the specific feeling is.

There are many ways that you can utilise eye accessing patterns and I will cover some of them later. For now, I would like you to begin to become aware of them happening in every day life.

The intention of the following exercise is to provide an opportunity for you to discover eye accessing patterns for yourself, by asking certain types of questions that require the listener to do a specific function in their mind and watching where their eyes move as they find the answer.

Experiment with your family, friends and colleagues.

Make sure that, for each 'type' of question, you work with at least three different people so that you can begin to notice the patterns that are consistent.

If they are happy to play along without knowing why you are asking them what you are asking them, you are more likely to get a clear result.

As soon as they know you are watching their eyes they will become consciously aware of their eyes and it will affect the results.

If you can ask the questions below, or similar questions that have the same effect, in natural conversation the results will be even clearer.

You can tackle the six types of questions below in any order. I would suggest that you stick to each one type of question until you have experienced a repetitive result.

Below is a representation of a face. Simply ask the types of question below that require the listener to create a certain type of representation in their mind. Watch where the listener's eyes go as they find the answer and mark the direction of eye movement on the face using the descriptions suggested below.

It is no coincidence that there are six types of question and six directional arrows.

1.   Ask questions that require the listener to remember a specific sound.

     Ask the person to remember the following and actually hear them:

     •   What does Tony Blair's voice sound like?
     •   What does Donald Duck's 'quack' sound like?
     •   Can you remember what Queen's *Bohemian Rhapsody* sounds like?
     •   What does a passing train sound like?
     •   Can you remember the theme tune to The A-Team?

Mark the direction of the eyes on the smiley face as A^R – Auditory Recall.

Construct your own 'natural' versions of these questions that will require the listener to remember a specific sound:

_____

_____

_____

2. Ask questions that require the listener to imagine/create a specific visual image.

    Ask the person to create an imaginary image for the following:

    - What would your car look like if it were green with red stripes?
    - Can you imagine a blue and orange tree?
    - Can you imagine a giant red cat?
    - What would a rainbow look like in black and white?
    - What would your living room look like if the TV were 3 metres wide?

    Mark the direction of the eyes on the smiley face as V^C – Visual Construct.

    Construct your own 'natural' versions of these questions that will require the listener to imagine a specific image:

    _____

    _____

    _____

3. Ask questions that require the listener to get a feeling.

    Ask the person to get a feeling sensation for the following:

    *   Can you get the feeling of sand in your hands and running through your fingers?
    *   How does your foot feel against your shoe?
    *   How does the sun feel on your back on a hot summer day?
    *   What does a cold shower feel like?
    *   What does a wet dog feel like?

    Mark the direction of the eyes on the smiley face as **K** – Kinaesthetic.

    Construct your own 'natural' versions of these questions that will require the listener to have a specific feeling:

    _____

    _____

    _____

4. Ask questions that require the listener to reason using the voice in their head.

    Ask the person to think about:

    *   Name the parts of the body that only have 3 letters.
    *   Name the countries that end in 'L'.
    *   Do your 7 x table in your head:... 1x7=7... 2x7=14... etc.
    *   Say a nursery rhyme in your head.
    *   How many times is the word 'up' used in 'The Grand Old Duke of York'?

    Mark the direction of the eyes on the smiley face as $\mathbf{A}^{D}$ – Auditory Digital.

    Construct your own 'natural' versions of these questions that will require the listener to go inside their head and reason something through:

_____

_____

_____

5. Ask questions that require the listener to imagine/create a specific sound and really hear it.

    Ask the person to imagine hearing the following:

    • What would my voice sound like if I were underwater?
    • What would your National Anthem sound like at 3x the speed?
    • What would George Bush sound like if he were a woman?
    • If you dropped a bag of sugar in a swimming pool what sound would it make?
    • What would a rubbish/garbage bin rolling down a hill sound like?

    Mark the direction of the eyes on the smiley face as A^c – Auditory Construct.

    Construct your own 'natural' versions of these questions that will require the listener to imagine a specific sound:

    _____

    _____

    _____

6. Ask questions that require the listener to remember a specific visual image.

    Ask the person to clearly picture:

    • What was the view from the window of the last hotel you stayed in?
    • What did your first bicycle look like?

74

- What did your first teacher/boss look like?
- What did the sleeve of the first album you bought look like?
- What does the poster for your favourite movie look like?

Mark the direction of the eyes on the smiley face as V^R – Visual Recall.

Construct your own 'natural' versions of these questions that will require the listener to remember a specific image:

_____

_____

_____

Did you see it?

If you practised with a few participants you were probably able to identify the consistent eye movements, the ones that they all did.

You may have noticed with some people that they always look in one place first, and then their eyes move to other places.

When this happens you are noticing their 'lead' representational system. It's the representational system that they access first, before then going to the relevant place.

You may be asking 'why we are covering this?', 'what does this have to do with connecting with people?' or 'how does this make a difference?'

Generally, we all use all of our representations systems. The idea is that we have favourite or preferred ones that we use more dominantly.

This preferred way of representing the world around us will be exhibited in our behaviour and, because people like alike people, we will be drawn to people who have the same dominant representation system that we do.

They will be behaving in a way that is 'like us'.

One of the indications of a preferred representation system is that we will use the eye patterns that correspond to that system more frequently.

This means that we can begin to notice when people are accessing a particular eye pattern frequently, and therefore what representation system they are using the most.

There is a degree of skill in noticing when people are choosing a favoured system. If you ask someone to describe what something looks like they will often use their visual representational system, obviously this does not mean that they favour their visual representation system, it's just what they are using to perform that task.

There are also other behaviours that indicate the frequent use of a preferred representation system. The utilisation of these behaviours as well as eye patterns will allow you to create a connection with people quickly and easily, and communicate in a way that will reduce resistance and eliminate misunderstanding.

Before we move on, I know you are wondering what your preferred representation system is...

How do you do it?

Please rank the following answers from 1 to 4, where 1 = least like you, and 4 = most like you. Allocate a number to all four letters. Use each number 1, 2, 3 or 4 only once per question. Go with your first instinct.

1. I like my home environment to be:
A __ Tidy looking
B __ Filled with the sounds I like
C __ Comfortably furnished
D __ Well organised

2. When listening I make judgements about people based upon:
A __ My gut feeling
B __ If I can see their point of view
C __ Their tone and if it sounds right
D __ If the facts make sense

3. When describing something I like to:
A __ Paint a picture
B __ Evoke a feeling
C __ Communicate effectively
D __ Tell a story

4. I am most influenced by people when:

A __ I understand what they mean

B __ I feel that I 'get it'

C __ I see their point of view

D __ I really hear what they are saying

5. I communicate myself by:

A __ The way I look

B __ The feelings I share

C __ The words I choose

D __ My tone of voice

6. I am:

A __ Very attuned to the sounds around me

B __ Quick to rationalise new facts or data

C __ Very sensitive to the way my clothes feel

D __ Immediately responsive to colours and appearances

Sudoku?

Each question on the previous page is represented by a horizontal row on the table below. Simply write the values you allocated to each letter A, B, C & D in the box with the corresponding letter.

So, for example:

Whatever number you allocated to 'B' on question 2 – "If I can see their point of view." – Write that number in the same box as the large letter 'B' in row 2 as shown by the #:

2	B #	C	A	D

1	A	B	C	D
2	B	C	A	D
3	A	D	B	C
4	C	D	B	A
5	A	D	B	C
6	D	A	C	B
Total ↓				
	V	A	K	Ad

What does it mean?

Perhaps the previous test has revealed one very clearly dominant function, or perhaps the functions were a little more evenly matched.

As you continue to work through this section you will become more and more aware of your favoured processing style and the results that you are getting from operating that way.

For now, I would like to begin to describe the behaviours that are associated with an individual using each dominant function.

As I provide these descriptions, make a note of people who you would instinctively place into each category. These could be people who you know or perhaps famous people who you have often seen on television.

The definitions below are exaggerated, 'archetypal' descriptions of people who are heavily biasing one representation system.

I would like to point out that this is not a psychometric test. It is not, nor does it claim to be, absolute or universal. As you can imagine, people use their different representation systems with different amounts of bias, and this slightly changes with a change of context, activity or state.

It has simply been observed that; if an individual processes the world a certain way internally, then the behavioural effects of that processing style seem to be fairly consistent with certain behaviours as described below.

There is an art to recognising and utilising these patterns. Rather than a 'black and white pigeon holing' exercise, it is an awareness of behavioural tendencies that take into account an enormous and varied amount of signals.

Think of this as something that people 'are doing' rather than something that people 'are'.

For now simply ask yourself, instinctively, do you recognise the following characteristics in people who you know well. Make a note of these people in the space provided.

V: Visual

People who favour using their visual representation system often have very upright body language. They sit forward with their back straight or stand quite 'erect'. They are often slim.

If you observe the movement of their chest you will see that they are breathing from the top of their lungs. They 'tend to be' organized, neat, well-groomed and orderly.

Their eye patterns will frequently move into 'visual' processing.

They often have trouble remembering verbal instructions because they are making pictures of what you are saying rather than remembering the words.

They will be interested in how things look. Appearances are important to them.

This description reminds me of:

_____

A: Auditory

People who favour using their auditory representational system will often have fairly neutral body language. They breathe from the middle of their chest.

They typically talk to themselves, and can be easily distracted by noise. *(Some even move their lips when they read or talk to themselves)*.

They often have a 'sing song' voice and *r-e-a-l-l-y* emphasize certain words.

Their eye patterns will frequently move into 'auditory' processing – they may achieve this by looking straight ahead and slightly moving their head slowly from side to side.

They can repeat things back to you easily, learn by listening.

The auditory person will usually like music and talking on the phone. They are sensitive to tone of voice or certain sets of words; sounds are important to them.

This description reminds me of:

_____

K: Kinaesthetic

People who favour using their kinaesthetic representational system usually have a relaxed or 'laid back' body language.

They will be breathing from the bottom of their lungs, so you'll see their stomach go in and out when they breathe.

They move and talk slowly and often have a smoother, deeper voice. They are sensitive to touch and will stand closer to people than a visual person.

Their eye patterns will often move to access 'feelings'.

They will be interested in how things feel.

This description reminds me of:

A^d: Auditory Digital

Rather than a favouring representation system that is a sense (V, A or K) people who favour Auditory Digital in communicating are using their 'Linguistic map' to 'make sense of' their experience.

They will use analytical or reporting language and want to know or understand things.

Their eye patterns will often move to access 'inner dialogue'.

The auditory digital person will still tend to exhibit characteristics of the other sensory based representational systems with varying amounts of bias.

This description reminds me of:

I see what you are saying...

One of the clearest indicators of a person's favoured representational system is shown by their predicates of speech.

Visual people will tend to choose visual words (see, look). Auditory people will tend to say auditory words (hear, sounds), Kinaesthetic people will use feeling words (feel, touch) and Auditory digital people will tend to think of inner reasoning words (know, understand).

This is important for several reasons: Have you ever, when travelling in a foreign country, attempted to speak the local language in 'pidgin' fashion? The mere gesture of attempting to speak in another person's language tends to make them extremely friendly and co-operative. Have you ever seen the tourist who, when his words are not understood, says the same thing slower and louder? What effect does that have?

When you develop the behavioural flexibility to change some of your word usage to compliment the other person's use of words, you will be 'speaking their language'. This creates rapport and a feeling of agreement or shared understanding; you would say that you are seeing things the same way.

Have you ever had a conversation with someone and agreed on the points you were discussing, yet not had the feeling of agreement? It felt like 'hard work'.

In my experience, this is caused by a difference in communication styles and a large part of this is often a 'clash' between the different representational systems being used.

Below are some everyday expressions. They are grouped into the area of processing style where they are most likely to be used; so the visual expressions will be favoured by the people favouring their visual representational system.

Because these are everyday expressions, people will use all of them at some time or another, and they will favour (use more often) the ones that are in line with their internal representations.

Have a look at how expressions below sound and get a feeling for which ones you understand and would use more frequently.

Notice the use of sensory words, which of your senses those sensory experiences relate to and how we have grouped them:

Visual

- Get a perspective
- In light of / In view of
- Looks like
- Catch a glimpse
- Take a peek
- Look into it
- Make a scene
- See to it

Auditory

- Have a chat
- To tell the truth

- Loud and clear
- Unheard of
- Utterly
- Strikes a chord
- Voiced an opinion
- Word for word
- Rings a bell

Kinaesthetic

- Concrete evidence
- Boils down to
- Cool/calm/collected
- Get to grips with
- Hold it!
- Hot headed
- Hold on a minute
- Heated argument
- Pull some strings
- I get it

Auditory Digital

- Makes sense
- I understand
- Perfectly logical
- It all adds up
- I know what you mean
- Afterthought
- Give an account of

You can clearly place words into categories by simply asking yourself which of the senses you would be using when you perform that sensory function.

For Example:

View	V	Listen	A	Grasp	K	Experience	A^d

You view with your eyes (V); listen with your ears (A), grasp something using you sense of touch in your hand (K) and define something as an experience in your linguistic map (A^d).

Here are some more examples:

Know	A^d	Touch	K	Look	V	Sound	A
See	V	Hear	A	Understand	A^d	Feel	K

Now it's your turn. Place the words below into the appropriate sensory category (V, A, K or A^d) as per the examples above:

Say		Appear		Think		Solid	
Tell		Learn		Hard		Show	
Process		Tune out		Reveal		Unfeeling	
Scrape		Decide		Harmonious		Bright	
Clear		Silence		Deduct		Concrete	
In Touch		Foggy		Consider		Resonate	
Perspective		Focused		Catch On		All Ears	
Hazy		Push		Deaf		Distinct	
Tap Into		Unhearing		Brilliant		Crystal	
Be heard		Question		Picture		Throw Out	

Lost in Translation

In this next exercise, you can begin to develop some flexibility in the words that you choose.

For each of the sentences below, identify the representation system being used, and then re-write the sentence 3 times, each time translated into the language of one of the other representation systems:

For example:

I can **see** this is easier than it first **looks.**   *Visual*

> 1. *I get the feeling this is not so tough.*
> 2. *I would say this is easier than it sounds at first.*
> 3. *I know this is easier than I first thought.*

I hear what you are saying.

_____

_____

_____

I feel that I will get a lot from doing this course.

_____

_____

_____

Analyse the information and report back to me.

_____

_____

_____

84

Answer the question...

One of the easiest ways to begin to bring this flexibility into your speech is to be mindful of how you are asked a question, and respond appropriately.

Consider this example:

Q. How do you feel about these changes?
A. I think it will be good.
A. They look good to me.
A. They sound like the right thing.

In all three cases, you have answered their question in your style not theirs; so you have not really answered their question. You have provided an answer in the same context on the same topic that is a correct response to the question as you received it, but not as they asked it.

Now consider the following by comparison:

Q. How do you feel about these changes?
A. I feel they will be good.

They have asked how you feel and you have answered that question exactly.

This will lead to an increased rapport between you and the other person, and they will feel that you are communicating well with each other.

Now your turn. feed back answers to these questions in the same sensory language that they are asked:

What do you think about London hosting the Olympic Games?

_____

What is your view on London hosting the Olympic Games?

_____

What would you say about London hosting the Olympic Games?

_____

How do you feel about London hosting the Olympic Games?

Spell Check; Language Check; Send.

Another way of beginning to use more flexible sensory language is in your written communication.

Emails are often quite informal and conversational, allowing you a lot of flexibility in your responses.

Because the words on an email you receive are static, it allows you plenty of time to observe the choice of words used in the emails you receive. It's then very easy to change a few of your words to make your reply even more agreeable to the recipient.

When you will begin to do this now you will be amazed how it alters the perception of the recipient, and therefore the meanings and intentions they put on your words. The responses you get as a result tend to be very convincing.

The following four pages contain the same message written four different ways.

The main point of the message is that the sender does not have time to meet with you.

Write a reply urging the sender to make time to meet with you soon, and write it 'in their language'. In other words, what ever sensory language you see in their email, write a reply that you feel will be most like the words they use.

Notice which of the four replies is easiest to write, and which is the most difficult:

> It was good to see an email from you today.
>
> I will have a look at your website and see what we can do with you.
>
> As you can imagine, my diary looks very busy, so I'm not sure if I can see you soon. When we do see each other, we will have to look at pricing.

It was good to talk yesterday.

It sounds like we have something to talk about, although I can't say when.

My diary is crazy so we will have to play it by ear. Does that sound OK? When we do have another chat, we will have to talk about price.

Thank you for getting in touch yesterday.

I get the feeling we will be able to work together.

I can't give you a firm date at the moment as my diary packed full. When we do get together I will need to get some concrete pricing from you.

Thank you for your communication of yesterday.

I think that there is certainly a possibility and I need to know more.

I have little available time to discuss this at the moment. When we do address this, I will need to analyse some figures before we can proceed.

When speaking, in addition to the words that you choose, your voice tone and speed of speech will make an enormous difference to rapport.

Have you ever had the experience of dealing with someone on the phone and found that:

- Their speech is so slow you get frustrated and begin to finish their sentences for them?
- Their voice tone 'goes right through you'?
- They speak so abruptly and quickly that it feels like an attack?

This mismatch of speaking styles is usually due to a mismatch of primary representation systems.

The common indications of favoured representation system in voice tone are:

Visual	Quick speech, sometimes in short bursts, often slightly louder or quieter than normal.
Auditory	Sing song voice with lots of expression and marking some words with expressive sounds.
Kinaesthetic	Slower, smooth, often deeper voice. Speech is often breathy.

Perhaps you can take a moment to think of people who you know who fit into these descriptions...

What do I do with this?

To conclude this section, the utilisation of favoured (primary) representation systems is a bit of an art.

If this is being brought into your consciousness for the first time, it may be a little bit difficult to notice primary representation systems in some real-life situations. The question I am often asked is, "How can I pay attention to all of these things and still have a conversation?"

Relax; it becomes very easy in time, especially if you will be attending a practitioner training course. You will soon reach a level of conscious competence with this.

When you are at the stage of conscious competence it may be an effort to see these things that are happening right in front of you.

To effectively utilise this pattern, like any other pattern, you will need to reach a level of unconscious competence, when you can do it automatically and without thinking about it.

For now – practise, practise, practise. Open your eyes and ears so that you can get to grips with what's going on around you...

Firstly, practising this, in whatever context you feel comfortable, will demonstrate to you how strangely powerful this pattern is.

Secondly, practice will allow you to reach the first level of conscious competence. This is important as this pattern, like most of the patterns of NLP, will not be effective without a level of comfort and skill in delivering them.

The following page outlines specific tasks and activities that will help to make application of these patterns easier on a day-to-day basis.

What I need to see/talk about/get is...

I would also urge you to consider what people need in order to effectively connect with what you are describing.

For many years I was the Managing Director of a design agency, and I cringe when I think back to the way I would present certain concepts or ideas.

On some occasions my presentations were very effective, and on others less so.

Imagine the potential consequence of: Showing a visual with no conversation of the rationale behind it; discussing a rationale without visual information; describing a quality paper finish and not providing a sample for the client to touch and feel; using a slide presentation of facts and figures without a visual mock-up or physical example.

In many cases the client will tell you exactly what sensory process they need satisfied – it will be predicated through their language.

If you are explaining or presenting something, ask yourself: Do you need to provide something to look at or visualise, to explore or explain with a conversation, to provide an experience and something to connect with or to furnish them with facts and data?

Homework

Find the preferred (primary) representation systems of at least three people using the chart below to gather evidence:

Name	Word usage	Voice tone	Body language	Primary Rep System

Practise changing your spoken language and body language to match the representation systems of others.

Watch a chat show or sports/entertainment programme and identify the preferred representation styles of the celebrities.

Begin to change your emails to match the word usage of the person you are communicating with.

When you interact with another person, experiment with changing your body language to be more like theirs – upright, neutral or laid back.

When you interact with another person, experiment with the speed and tone of your voice to be more like theirs – quick, expressive or slow.

I would like to end this section with a 'Big Idea' about behaviour:

Some time ago I was working as a director of a small and extremely busy business. After a year or so of working together, one of my co-directors began to behave in an unusual way. (For the purpose of the story that may not even be true I'm going to call him Dave).

Even though he lived a couple of minutes walk from the office, Dave would usually arrive slightly late in the morning, take a long lunch break and always leave on time at the end of the day.

Dave did not have the kind of job where he needed to 'clock in' – his hours were his to keep as he saw fit and he was evaluated purely on his results.

However, the consequence of Dave's timekeeping was that the rest of the team would be slightly impeded by absences and they would need to do more to 'take up the slack'. They would need an urgent piece of information and Dave was not there. They would try to contact Dave and find his mobile phone was switched off.

I thought I had best address this, so during an informal conversation I introduced the topic of timekeeping and was surprised by Dave's 'out of character' reaction. He went slightly red in the face and he said it was none of my business. He said he had a life outside of the office and as long as he was meeting his commercial objectives I should 'back off'.

After our conversation Dave's timekeeping became worse and, although Dave was liked by the team, they began to perceive him as a bit selfish. After a while he earned himself a nickname. They began to call him 'selfish Dave' when he was not around.

I still remember the day, a few weeks later, when it was brought to my attention that, at that time, Dave was a full time carer for a disabled relative.

He stopped being 'selfish' Dave very, very quickly.

As humans we tend to make the mistake of observing the behaviour of another person, making some kind of value judgement about that behaviour and then attributing that meaning to the person's entire character.

For example: You may observe a person behaving in a certain way that you decide is 'rude'.

(By the way; I have no idea what that word means – what is rude to one person is not rude to another – the word has no definition, it's a value judgement, it's whatever you decide it is. As such – rudeness does not really exist.)

You then attribute the rude behaviour to their entire character, saying something like, "they are a rude person".

Are they really? All the time? Are they rude to everyone they know? Or are they just behaving in a rude way right now?

I'm sure that you are aware your behaviour is different in one context than in another. Perhaps your behaviour is different when you are working to how you behave when you are socialising or doing your hobby.

Have you ever had the experience of driving on the fast lane of a major road when a car approaches you quickly from behind, flashing their lights at you and driving too close to your rear bumper? When this happens to me I glance down to the dashboard and look at my speed, and upon discovering that I am travelling at the speed limit or slightly over it, I call the person in the car behind a name, and it's not a very nice name. I don't know what name you have for a person in this scenario.

Then I stop myself and think – he could be on his way to a hospital. I have no idea what context is driving his current behaviour, yet the tendency is to make a judgement about it.

We have as many behaviours as we have contexts and experiences.

We have all had bad days at some time in the past – I'm sure you have behaved in the past in a way that is not really like your typical behaviour. Someone could have observed that behaviour and made one of these Fundamental Attribution Errors, deciding that behaviour was who you are. Of course, it's not.

I do quite a lot of coaching. If I believed that people were their behaviours, what could I possibly do to help them? I would have to say, "Well, that's just what they are like, nothing I can do." Effective coaching would be impossible on this basis. I would not get much repeat business if I believed people were their behaviours.

We are complicated creatures. I would urge you to resist the temptation to label people in any way. Do not make judgements about their character; do not put them in boxes based upon their response to any particular stimulus.

People are beautifully sophisticated, complicated and inconsistent animals. All you know about the person you are working with is the sensory information you can observe from their responses, remembering that those responses may be different if the context is changed, so they are temporary and do not convey any reliable 'meaning'.

And that's all you need to know in order to begin to become an exceptional communicator…

Summary

- Based upon observation, we are assuming that 'People like alike people'.

- We have different sensory systems for experiencing the world, and favour some of these representational systems more than others.

- These preferences are observable in our verbal and non-verbal communication.

- You can create rapport and improve the quality of you interactions with others if you 'speak their language' and match their behaviour.

- Behaviour operates context-dependently; so perhaps 'people are more than their behaviours'.

An interesting topic

I find it surprising how many people show an interest in the fascinating study of body language, yet they seldom pay attention to it.

It's especially surprising as it's such an easy thing to become aware of – there are great examples going on right in front of you all of the time.

You can start again!

I would invite you, with some guidance from this chapter, to begin to pay attention to the body language communication that has eluded you in the past.

There are some studies of body language that define what a certain gesture 'means'. These studies are interesting, entertaining and based upon accurate study. However; there are so many subtleties in body language and idiosyncratic behaviours that vary from one individual to another that such explicit interpretations are extremely unreliable. The most common example is allocating a meaning to someone having their 'arms crossed' as a 'defensive' gesture when they could just be cold or something else.

Certainly, your gestures are linked to your thought processes. And you can begin to become aware of certain non verbal signals. *Remember the Big Idea: mind & body inevitably and inescapably affect each other.*

However the meaning of particular gestures is not specific, just as words are not specific – they are more of a process – and it's not possible to know what that process 'means' in explicit terms.

To illustrate this point I would like to draw your attention to the one type of non-verbal communication that we are very aware of – facial expressions.

We can notice facial expressions with some degree of accuracy, but it is not an exact science. For example, you know what a frown is, you know what it looks like, you are able to 'label' a particular facial expression as a frown – but you have no idea what the frown 'means'.

There are a huge variety of frowns and people could frown for a multitude of reasons – confusion, irritation, frustration, doubt, etc. When someone frowns, all you know is that they have tensed certain muscles in their face, creating an expression that you would label as a frown. The moment you begin to 'mind read' that you know what the frown means or why they are frowning you are deluding yourself. You simply cannot know this without asking.[*]

Rather than labelling certain body languages postures and allocating meaning to them, we will be looking at the dynamic of body language that we can utilise to make a difference to our communication?

You are more sensitive to the body language of others than you realise. You respond to non verbal gestures from others without being consciously or explicitly aware of their meaning.

My intention in this section is to provide a coupe of contexts for discovery. I'm going to set you some 'people watching' homework.

Your task is to observe people in very agreeable situations:

- Friends at a bar.
- People at the end of a dinner party.
- A team (who get on well) on their 'tea break'.

What do you notice about their body language in relation to each other? Is it similar or different? How?

_____

_____

Now notice people who are in conflict, or resistant to each other, or that do not like each other.

- An uncomfortable meeting.
- A customer complaining in a shop.

Is it similar or different? How?

_____

_____

---

[*] Except – There has been extensive research into modelling facial expressions that isolates the use of specific muscles, or combinations of muscles, and has linked them to particular internal processes or 'states'. There are some people who, as a result of extensive research can visually identify these extremely specific expressions and quite reliably label them with the corresponding internal process. Unless you have spent years studying in such detail, It is resourceful to remind yourself that you do not know what non verbal communication 'means' and prevent yourself from 'mind reading'.

There are three skills that I believe are most fundamental to the Practitioner of NLP – the ability to calibrate on the physiological changes in the person you are communicating with, the ability to utilize whatever they provide you with and the ability to create and maintain an unconscious rapport between you and them.

Calibration skills are not covered in this workbook as they are, in my opinion, best learned from a context of discovery and experience; there is little you can learn from me telling you about it.

The NLP method of creating rapport is easier to define.

When people are in rapport, they will behave in a similar way.

By the end of a dinner party, all of the guests usually adopt the same body language.

It's what happens naturally. If you are reading this in a public place, look around; is there anyone else in the same posture?

When people who are 'getting on' walk along the street together, they will walk 'in step' with each other. People in rapport will lift their cups of coffee, glasses of wine or pints of beer simultaneously with no conscious awareness of doing so.

People in rapport 'become like each other' physiologically.

So you can use this natural process to accelerate the feeling of 'getting on' by adopting the same 'type' of body language as the other person.

This may seem like a strange claim – surely it can't be that simple. All I need to do is adopt a similar body language to the other person and they will like me? No way.

Well, to some degree it's true. If you adopt the same body language you will be capturing the unconscious attention of the other person and often creating an 'agreeable' atmosphere.

The reaction of the other person can vary. If someone has an 'issue' with the communication, they will be uncomfortable being comfortable, and shift to a different body language when you match them. By the way, this is a great 'acid test'.

You know you have rapport when you can lead the other person; after a few minutes of the matching condition, mismatch your body language and see if the other person moves with you. If they do, rapport has been achieved.

The only way to understand this is to experience it. I suggest that you experiment with your body language in relation to others, behaving like them, and see what happens. Notice how the 'atmosphere' between you feels more positive. Then see if you can begin to lead them.

When there is no rapport, or even conflict the opposite is true, there will be distinctly different body languages. The other person will find it difficult to be resistant to you when you are in rapport, so if they intend to be resistant, they will break rapport and make their physiology different to yours.

A great example of this was provided to me in a recent training session. I was working for a major UK bank and one of the attendees had recently been involved in a meeting in New York:

He described how he was presenting an idea to a partnering Manhattan bank and he used the words, "We have put together a scheme." At the moment he said those words all of the American participants in the room suddenly shifted their posture. Luckily he was aware enough of this change to realise the communication may have gone off track and he asked, "Is that not what you expected?"

After further investigation it transpired that although the word 'scheme' simply means a plan in the UK, in the US it's something far more sinister – it means underhanded or 'scheming'.

In this case awareness of the change in the body language condition prevented a huge misunderstanding.

This brings me on to another Big Idea:

Resistance indicates a lack of Rapport

And, as in the story above, a break of rapport indicates resistance.

Take a moment to think of some situations where people have been resistant to your ideas or opinions.

Now imagine the same situation and substitute the other person with your best friend. Can you imagine your best friend being deliberately resistant?

If you create the right level of rapport, it is extremely difficult for the other person to be resistant toward you. Therefore, if they manage to be resistant, the right level of rapport has not been achieved or the effect is being weakened by another aspect of your non-verbal communication or voice tone.

As your rapport skills become more developed, you can even create rapport with anyone extremely quickly, using your body language to create and maintain an agreeable atmosphere.

VAK Physiology

We know from earlier that 'People like alike people' and that primary representation systems will be reflected in your behaviour. It has been suggested that there is a type of body language that generally relates to people who favour certain representation systems. I find this to be fairly helpful in identifying and matching representation systems; and not entirely reliable so please base any judgements on more observation than this alone.

Visual	Upright body language. Breathe from top of chest.
Auditory	Neutral body language. Breathe from middle of chest.
Kinaesthetic	Very relaxed body language. Breathe from belly.

When you begin to adapt your behaviour to compliment the behaviour of the other person, by having comfortable flexibility of body language, you can make a strong connection extremely quickly.

Handy tricks

Here's an interesting bit of psychology that first came to my attention in another of Malcolm Gladwell's books, *The Tipping Point* (2000). Gladwell describes a fascinating experiment carried out by the social scientists Gary Wells and Richard Petty at Ohio State University:

A large group of students were recruited for what they were told was a market-research study by a company making high-tech headphones. They were each given a headset and told that the company wanted to test to see how well they worked when the listener was in motion – dancing up and down, say, or moving his or her head. All of the students *listened to songs by Linda Ronstadt and the Eagles, and then heard a radio editorial arguing that tuition at their university should be raised from its present level of $587 to $750.*

A third were told that while they listened to the taped radio editorial they should nod their heads vigorously up and down. The next third were told to shake their heads from side to side. The final third were the control group. They were told to keep their heads still. When they were finished, all the students were given a short questionnaire, asking them questions about the quality of the songs and the effect of the shaking. Slipped in at the end was the question the experimenters really wanted an answer to: "What do you feel would be an appropriate dollar amount for undergraduate tuition per year?"

The students who kept their heads still were unmoved by the editorial. The tuition amount that they guessed was appropriate was $582 – or just about where tuition was already. Those who shook their heads from side to side as they listened to the editorial ... disagreed strongly with the proposed increase. They wanted tuition to fall on average to $467 a year. Those who were told to nod their heads up and down, meanwhile, found the editorial very persuasive. They wanted tuition to rise, on average, to $646.

I think that the above experiment suggests that the act of nodding links to a state – a state of agreement that contains the nodding as a component part of the subject's physiology. This would certainly support observation from practising NLP and calibrating on unconscious responses to yes/no questions.

After further investigation I found the following similar study that was recently published in the Journal of Personality and Social Psychology:

Richard Petty recruited 82 subjects to conduct this study. In order to hide the real purpose of the experiment, the subjects were again told that they would be assessing the sound quality of headphones. Half of the group was instructed to nod while the other half were told to shake their heads.

The subjects then listened to one of two radio shows. Both featured music and an editorial advocating university ID cards. In one recording, the host gave a strong, logical argument in favour of student IDs. In the other, the presenter gave an unpersuasive argument for them. Afterward, participants were asked how they felt about the headphone quality and – by the way – were asked what they thought about university ID cards.

The study concluded that nodding increases confidence in your own thoughts or opinions whether they are positive or negative. Shaking your head has the opposite effect; undermining your own opinion.

This study suggests that nodding increases confidence in positive thoughts as more participants who nodded agreed with the strong and logical argument than those who shook their heads. [*]

However, a new development is the suggestion that those who heard the unpersuasive arguments showed the reverse pattern. These students agreed less with the message when they were nodding than when shaking. The conclusion drawn is that nodding movements also seem to increase confidence in the negative thoughts they had to the poor arguments compared to shaking.

This last conclusion that nodding increases confidence in negative thoughts is where the content imposition goes too far for me – and it is contrary to what I would conclude from the same information.

If we have observed that the act of nodding is an affirmative internal process – we have now added the contradictory conclusion that could, maybe, if the wind is blowing in the right direction, also be a negative process.

Here's a simpler explanation: If we preserve the idea that nodding is somehow affirmative, we have a condition where the listener is in an affirmative and congruent state, and the speaker delivering the unconvincing argument is indicating a deliberately incongruent state through voice tone and choice of words.

The miss-matching of these conditions between listener (thinking yes) and speaker (saying I'm not so sure) is likely to create a strong feeling of disagreement in the listener. Not because the nod could reinforce the negative; because the speaker's behaviour is miss-matching the affirmative mindset of the listener – the listener is likely to think contrary thoughts in the positive and reinforce them rather than thinking negative thoughts. In this case both results are explained by the physiology being a component part of the affirmative state rather than

---

[*] Personally, I think that the word 'confidence' is an imposition from the observer's frame of reference; how do they know the assertions of the subjects was a result of confidence specifically unless it came directly from the subjects' description?

101

one physiology being two different processes.

I have modelled this experiment with some colleagues (who were naive to the experiment) to satisfy my curiosity and I asked them to describe their experience of nodding to both delivery styles. Their comments support my conclusion.

Nodding is a very simple and powerful body language technique that you can use to put yourself into an affirmative and congruent mindset.

You can use nodding to take control of your thought processes. I wonder if you will allow me to demonstrate:

As you read this page, begin to nod in a comfortable affirmative way. It may be a large nod or a nearly invisible small nod, it could be fast or slow, whatever feels like a comfortable and natural nod.

Now, as you become comfortable with nodding, continuing to nod, try to have a negative thought.

If you followed the instructions above you will have found the negative thought difficult to find. We know that, just as our thoughts affect or physiology, our physiology affects our thoughts. Nodding would seem to 'flick a switch' in your mind.

When you nod at someone, they will be tempted to nod back. It's almost irresistible, and when they nod back at you they are switching their mind into positive.

The same is true of smiling. When you genuinely smile at someone, it's almost irresistible for them to smile back; they would need to make an effort not to. When they smile, the resultant positive change in their 'state' will be anchored to seeing you. Do it often enough and they will begin smiling at you first.

It's the simplest of things to do and so very powerful. It can completely change the world you live in. Don't take my word for it; smile and see what happens.

4. Investigative Listening
The Meta Model

An armada of the US Navy was engaged in naval exercises off the coast of Canada when the following radio exchange was recorded.

A: "Please divert your course 15 degrees to the north to avoid danger of collision."

B: "Recommend that you divert *your* course 15 degrees to the south to avoid danger of collision."

A: "We repeat, divert north now to avoid collision."

B: "Strongly recommend you divert south soonest to avoid mishap."

A: "This is the Captain of a US Navy warship. I say again, divert your course with immediate effect."

B: "Copy, we say divert south." ·

A: *"This is the USS Enterprise. We are an aircraft carrier of the US Navy. Divert your course NOW!"*

B: "We are a Canadian lighthouse – your call."

(Primary source – The Daily Telegraph)

Are words a blessing or a curse?

So you are probably wondering about listening. You may be thinking "surely I do listen, otherwise how would I be able to reply?" or "my friends say I'm a good listener".

Have you ever heard the words "That's not what I said", "I didn't mean that" or "You are missing my point"? Have you ever been presented with an account of something that didn't quite add up – you felt something was missing and you couldn't see what it was?

We naturally learn to listen on a surface level, and there can be times when it is best to do so. However, listening on a surface level provides opportunities for misunderstandings.

You can learn to listen at a deeper level, allowing you to gather more precise information, get a more accurate overall picture and hear where the speaker is leaving details out of their descriptions – providing you with their version of events and influencing you with their assumed meaning.

The ability to gather more information will quite obviously help you in just about every business activity. How much easier is it to sell something to someone if you know what, when and how they want to buy? How much easier is it to motivate someone when you know what motivates them? How much easier will it be to interact with others on projects when you can hear exactly what they are saying, and what they are leaving out?

In order to understand what is really being said, as well as what's not being said, and how words affect our minds, we need to understand what happens when we hear words as a listener.

When you listen to someone speaking, you use your values, opinions and experiences to add meaning to their words. The speaker has chosen their words based upon their own values, opinions and experiences, which will be different to yours; so the speaker's intended meaning may well be different to the meaning you put on the words when you receive them. That's how misunderstandings happen.

For example, if I were to say, "It's quite cool for a summer's day" there are a variety of meanings you could apply to that sentence.

Maybe I'm glad it's cool because it's been too hot, or I don't like the heat. Maybe I'm disappointed that it's cool because I love the summer heat. Obviously the way I say it and my tone of voice will indicate some meaning, however voice tone can easily be misread.

Also, what does 'quite cool' mean? If you want to do an experiment, give the word quite a rating out of ten. Then ask some other people how they would rate 'quite' out of ten. And ask them if 'quite' is a positive, or a negative word. You may be surprised at the variety of interpretations.

Quite cool compared to what? Compared to recent weather, compared to this time last year, compared to other countries in the Northern hemisphere? Who says it's quite cool? Is that from a temperature reading or the speaker's perception?

Most verbal descriptions are fairly vague, and as a listener we add meaning to them. For example, if I were to say, "Imagine a car", it's fairly obvious that we will be thinking of different cars.

Even when we add some more specific description there is still enormous latitude for the listener's interpretation to be very different from what the speaker is attempting to describe. If I were to say you "Imagine a green car", obviously we will probably still be imagining a different type of car, and what are the chances of us imagining exactly the same colour green? So even the more specific details can be ambiguous.

Spoken communication is ambiguous, and it contains relatively few details in relation to the complexity of what is being described.

In order to build an internal representation of what the speaker is telling us, we must add details whether they are pictures, sounds or feelings or logical thought processes.

Even when speech is quite descriptive, it invites you to imagine, and is not specific about how you imagine it, rather than communicating every little detail.

In searching for meaning and understanding, we 'colour in' the speaker's account, embellish upon what is said, adding in details so that we can imagine the scene that they are relaying to us.

When someone says, "It was a tall, modern building" we imagine a tall, modern building in our minds. Of course the building that we are imagining will be different to the building that the speaker is describing. To add meaning to and have understanding of the speaker's words, we need to imagine what *we **think*** they are communicating.

Most of the time we fool ourselves into thinking that we know exactly what the speaker means; this is almost impossible because of the amount of information that is missed out in the speaker's account.

If I were to say, "I was just being funny," you could easily attribute a meaning to those words. What did they really mean? Did I mean I was *only* being funny, or I was *recently* being funny, and did I mean funny – *humorous*, funny – *strange* or funny – *something else*?

The only way for your imagined reality to be very similar to the speaker's reality, is for the speaker to go into a painful amount of detail in their spoken description of things. Not only is it difficult to listen to speech containing an overwhelming amount of detail, it's also incredibly time consuming, and it will still be ambiguous because of the ambiguous and metaphoric nature of the words we use.

If someone attends a one-hour meeting and then reports back to you, that reporting back process will probably take 5 or 10 minutes. What about the other 50 minutes? Where did that go? It has been summarised, and in doing so an enormous amount of information has been missed out or distorted in some way.

As well as ambiguity and the variety of meaning given to words, there is something else that prevents us from listening properly:

If you are thinking of what you are about to say next, you are not really listening.

We discovered in an earlier section that different parts of our brain perform different tasks. The part of the brain used for listening is different to the part of the brain used for constructing speech, and if your attention is on thinking of what you will say next whilst someone is still talking, your ability to listen is diminished. Your attention direction is toward what you will say; not carefully interpreting what is being said.

So how does this relate to business? You will be making all communication activities easier for yourself when you accurately listen.

The more information you gather and the more you know, the easier it is to have the right answer, make the right suggestion and focus on the right area.

Gathering precise information equips you for selling, marketing, influencing or representing yourself appropriately in any context. When you learn what people need, or what is important to them, it's easy to make an agreeable and acceptable suggestion. When you get the right information the interaction will happen easily and effortlessly.

If you have not first investigated with listening and questioning, your suggestions will be 'guesses', and you can imagine what effect too many incorrect guesses will have.

For example; imagine that you need to provide a car for your colleague. What car would you suggest?

You would probably suggest the car that you think would be best for them; and they may not agree. What's important to them about their car will probably be different to what's important to you about your car. They may require different things that you have not considered and may not value things that you think are important.

We so often make suggestions based upon what we think is the best quality, most practical, most desirable, best value most suitable choice for the other person. The other person may not agree. After all, there are a lot of different cars on the road; and the other person is not you.

Now imagine that you need to provide a car for a colleague and you know that they like German engineering, need 4 or 5 doors for the kids, like fairly compact cars for around town, think fuel economy and the environment are important, and really like silver coloured cars.

How much easier is it to suggest a car now? If a car does not 'spring

108

to mind', you know what to look for.

How much easier is it to focus on the most appropriate aspects of your CV in an interview when you know exactly what role the employer company wants you to perform, how they want you to interact with others and the knowledge and experience they think are valuable.

Have you ever heard the expression "you have two ears and one mouth, and you should use them in that proportion"?

I personally do quite a bit of executive coaching and have been fortunate to work with several very capable, experienced and senior people from large organisations. One of the most consistent things that I find is; the more senior and successful the individual, the more they value listening properly, and most of them wish they had learned to do it much earlier in their career.

Many people, in many circumstances reply as a knee-jerk reaction. They hear something and immediately comment. Others may just stop listening when they think they have heard enough. They may indicate this by saying something like, "Yeah, yeah, I know what you mean," or, "I know where this is going."

I have even seen people in senior positions immediately raise their hand, making a 'talk to the hand' style gesture and say, "Thank you, I know what you are going to say."

How can they possibly know? Are they using psychic powers? Even if we give them the benefit of the doubt, maybe 90% of the time they do know what that person is going to say – what about the other 10%? What about the additional information or different perspective that they are completely missing by cutting the other person off?

Also, how do you think the other person feels when you 'cut them off' or 'show them the hand'?

When you learn to use investigative listening you will remove your assumptions, take time to clarify what is being said and put a gap between stimulus and response, stopping the knee-jerk reactions and allowing you to choose more effective responses.

This gap between stimulus and response is what allows you to put your communication into the other person's language and use the influential language patterns you will discover in later chapters, so it's really important to learn to listen first.

It doesn't matter how influentially you speak, present and negotiate if you are talking about the wrong thing. You must listen first in order to choose the most effective way to speak.

As mentioned earlier, words mean different things to different people. If you did the experiment with the word 'quite' you will have noticed a variety of different perceptions.

That's because:

Meaning operates context-dependently

So words are unreliable!

We each have different meanings, feelings, experiences or processes attached to different words.

If you want to experiment with some more words use: 'nice', 'wicked' and 'a bit funny'. Perhaps you can think of a few more words or expressions that can mean different things to different people depending upon how they are said and in what context.

Last week someone told me that a coaching session was outstanding. I said, "Thank you for saying so." They said, "No – outstanding; you haven't done it yet!"

During the early 1990's I spent a couple of years living in Florida and travelled extensively during that time, working in many different States of America. Being typically English, I can sometimes have a subtle and dry sense of humour with plenty of irony and a bit of sarcasm. In Florida, what I thought were hilarious quips and 'one-liners' fell on deaf ears; the local people just didn't 'get it' – they would look at me blankly or quizzically; and then dismiss the comment as "stupid" or "rude".

I found many of the people who I met in Florida had a more literal listening style. They did 'get' irony and sarcasm; I just had to make it much more obvious with my voice tone and body language to indicate that I was making a joke.

In Los Angeles however, my subtle vocal inflections that indicate irony or sarcasm were recognised. The Californians I encountered were somehow more equipped to detect the subtle changes in my voice tone and allocate a meaning to them that seemed to be closer to my intended meaning.

Please excuse my hideous generalisation about people from different geographical areas, it is of course completely unfounded and unfair; I'm simply using some personal experience to illustrate a point. I learned that my words alone were completely unreliable. It depended upon what the listener heard and the meaning they put on my words.

Either way, when you think about it, even the supposition that the Californians 'understood' me is a bit unreliable. I have no way of knowing what meaning they allocated to my words without asking them, I can only guess based upon the way that they responded. Communication is not an exact science. If I tell a joke and someone laughs and has a positive reaction, that's good enough for me. I have no idea if they found it funny for exactly the same reason as I did.

If you work on email, as so many of us do, you have probably already realised how people can put a different meaning on your words.

Emails are read completely differently depending upon what you think the sender's attitude is.

My favourite real-life example of this took place a few years ago when I sent a one-word reply email to a member of my staff. It simply read, 'Great!'

I wrote it because I thought the email I received from them was great. No hidden meaning, just sincerely great. Some hours later the member of staff plucked up the courage to tell me that they were very upset by my brief, flippant and sarcastic email. I was stunned and confused by their reaction.

They did not think it was great. Their frame of reference was different. They expected me to be unhappy or disappointed, so the word 'Great!' took on a completely different meaning for them. On email, without voice tone or body language, words can be very, very unreliable.

A comprehensive and up-to-date English dictionary does not really help to solve this problem either. The dictionary is a wonderful thing because it provides us with a rich and varied language that we can use to share and communicate sophisticated ideas.

The dictionary is also a terrible thing because it provides us with the illusion that words are specific things with exact, qualified and quantifiable meanings.

The meaning of words and the way they are used can be very different to their dictionary definition, and the dictionary definition becomes irrelevant when you consider that the meaning of a word is

111

what someone takes it to be, not what the big fat book gathering dust on the bookshelf defines it to be.

I'm sure that you are aware how you can completely change the meaning of a word with your voice tone, making it sarcastic or ironic.

Language is alive, changing, complicated, sophisticated, instinctive, implicit, and its perceived meaning from the perspective of the listener is governed by context, voice tone and body language. When you add to this the fact that we define words differently and have different 'understanding' of a word, it's amazing that we communicate at all.

A simile that you may find useful if you have a basic understanding of computers is that language is like the software of our brain; our sensory information (VAKOG) is the operating system and our sensory organs and human system are the hardware. In talking to people about their 'problems' you will find that, in most cases, the hardware and operating system are fine – it's just 'bugs' in the software that lead to difficulties.

As we covered under the banner of 'The map is not the territory', most problems exist in the map, not in the territory.

Many of us do much of our internal thinking in words. Words are more than a definition, they are an internal process.

The 'linguistic map' in our mind is a function that develops as we grow and we learn the words that become allocated to that defining and comparative reasoning. We do not 'learn' language, we assimilate it. As a child we pick up phrases and later recognise the individual words that comprise them. We get a feel for their meaning as a result of the context that we experience them in and the non-verbal communication that accompanies them.

Ask yourself this, of your own enormous vocabulary, have you looked up and learnt an explicit definition for every word that you use? How do you know what they mean? It's an instinctive awareness of meaning that is conditioned by experience.

When you hear or read a word, you are required to allocate a meaning to that word in your mind. When you find a meaning, that meaning then begins to run a process in your mind. That's how some words are shocking. It's not the sound of the word itself that shocks you; it's the meaning you allocate to that word in your mind.

Other words may evoke other feelings. It's not the word that evokes the feeling; it's the meaning that you allocate to that word and the resultant process that you run.

Because the word evokes an internal process that associates it to a meaning, the dictionary definition of the word is not necessarily correct. So in spoken language, the meaning of a word is the meaning you allocate to it, or the process you run in your mind, not necessarily how the dictionary defines it.

Don't take my word for it – let's look at a couple of everyday words as examples:

Consider the word **'but'**:

We often use the word 'but' in a sentence to link two different or opposing things into the same point.

That is not what happens in your mind. Consider the difference between the two sentences below:

"Your performance is generally good *but* you need to work on your communication."

"Your performance is generally good *and* you need to work on your communication."

The word 'but' negates whatever came before it. When the listener hears the word 'but' they 'throw away' what has been said before it. They hear 'but' and think 'here it comes…'

By replacing the word 'but' with 'and' the listener hears the entire sentence.

As well as detracting from the first part of the sentence, the word 'but' also puts emphasis on the second part of the sentence.

Consider the difference between the following sentences:

"You didn't meet your target but your turnover is up by 10% on last year."

"Your turnover is up by 10% on last year but you didn't make your target."

By changing where the positive and negative points are in relation to the 'but' we change the perceived meaning of the sentence. The first sentence can be interpreted as; you didn't meet your target and that doesn't matter because your turnover is up 10%. The second sentence can be interpreted as; your turnover is up 10% and that doesn't matter because you still didn't make your target.

The listener will focus on the second half of the sentence, and perceive that as the point the speaker is emphasizing, so if the second part of the sentence is negative, that's what the listener will be taking from the exchange.

I would recommend that you **try** to avoid the word but, and that

113

would be pretty ineffective, bringing me on to my next unreliable word:

Have you ever considered what the speaker is thinking when they say **"Try"?**

If you were to look up the word 'try' in a dictionary you would read:

Try

- **verb (tries, tried) 1** make an attempt or effort to do something. **2** (also **try out**) test (something new or different) in order to see if it is suitable, effective, or pleasant. **3** attempt to open (a door), contact (someone), etc. **4 (try on)** put on (an item of clothing) to see if it fits or suits one. **5** make severe demands on. **6** subject (someone) to trial. **7** investigate and decide (a case or issue) in a formal trial.

- **noun** (pl. **tries**) **1** an effort to do something; an attempt. **2** an act of testing something new or different. **3** Rugby an act of touching the ball down behind the opposing goal line, scoring points and entitling the scoring side to a kick at goal.

- **phrases: tried and tested** (or **true**), having proved effective or reliable before; **try one's hand at,** attempt to do for the first time; **try it on,** British informal, deliberately test or attempt to deceive or seduce someone.

- **usage:** the constructions **try to** and **try and** (as in *we should try to (or try and) help them*) mean the same thing, but **try and** is more informal; use **try to** in formal writing or speech.

This definition becomes irrelevant when you realise that, in the listener's mind the word 'try' means 'fail'. The word only appears in the speaker's sentence with the possibility of not achieving what is said. If you knew that you were going to do something you would say 'I will'.

Compare the following two sentences:

"I will meet you there."

"I will **try** to meet you there."

The use of the word try indicates that the speaker is entertaining the possibility of not turning up. Otherwise, why would they say it?

In order to use the word 'try', the speaker must be unconsciously thinking of something that will prevent them from doing so.

When you use the word 'try' the listener may consciously think you have said that you will do your best, and unconsciously they will have heard that you are expecting to fail.

We are conditioned by experience. Usually when people have said, "I will try to..." they have not done whatever it was. So we are conditioned by experience to equate trying with failing.

I even use the word when I am playing games with hypnosis. If I want one of my willing friends to fail to do a simple task, I will tell them to "REALLY TRY!"

So **don't** use the word try – (although the word 'don't' is even less reliable).

Allow me to illustrate what I mean by that.

What would happen if I were to say to you, "Don't think of baked beans"?

You think of baked beans. You have to think of baked beans in order to know what you should not think of, so that you can then not think of them.

What does a child do when you say "Don't run", "Don't drop it" or "Don't touch"?

Your mind is incapable of immediately processing negatives. It has to do the positive first and then consciously turn it into a negative.

In the past some people have said to me that this does not work on them; that they do not think of baked beans. I ask them, how do you know? You have to have thought of what baked beans are, otherwise how do you know you are not thinking of them?

It's a completely unconscious process of awareness, and it is unavoidable.

Here's another example. As you read this paragraph, don't yawn. Don't imagine how it feels when you begin to yawn, and don't think of how strangely familiar and comfortable that yawning sensation is. Try not to yawn. I don't know if you will yawn now or if you have already yawned earlier in this paragraph or if you will yawn later on this page and, either way, when you will have yawned, even though you are trying not to yawn you can begin to notice that these words really work on an unconscious level.

So what happens in business when you say, "Don't worry" or "It's not a problem"? – The listener will immediately think about why they should worry or how it could be a problem. You are bringing into the listener's awareness the very thing that you wish to negate.

We are simply not able to think in the negative. We have to first consider the statement as if it were positive, and then turn it to the negative.

In this process we have done the positive bit first.

115

When someone says, "It's not a problem" – you immediately have to define what a problem is in your mind, thus you are thinking about what constitutes a problem, before you can apply the "it's not a" part of the sentence.

The conversation has been 'primed' within the 'frame' of problems before you start.

By now you should be beginning to realise that, when speaking and listening, the meaning of a word is not an exact thing, and it's not the dictionary definition that determines what a word means, it's the meaning that you allocate to the word in your mind, and different people will allocate different meanings to the same word.

Words are extremely unspecific so the meaning of a word can be influenced by values, opinions, past experiences, perceptions, preconceptions and listening styles to name just a few possible factors.

I hope that by now you are beginning to shake up your perception of 'correct or incorrect' meaning.

The only way we could live by dictionary definitions would be to further qualify many of the words in the dictionary, carry a copy of the dictionary with us at all times, remove any kind of tonality from or voices, and do away with sarcasm, irony and inferential speech.

I trust that, at this point you can begin to get a feel for how unreliable words are, see how meaning that is heard can differ for different people, and understand how we allocate meaning to words in our minds.

That means we can move on to hearing what is really being said by the speaker, what they are assuming, and what they are leaving out.

First we need to look at what assumptions you are making as a listener...

Are you a Mind Reader?

Before addressing the language model that we will be using for listening, you must first become aware of a very human habit that prevents you from listening impartially.

To understand what a speaker is attempting to communicate, we need to make a representation of it in our mind. Take a moment to think of how you do this. You probably thought of an 'internal representation' made of imagined pictures, sounds and feelings.

In order to create a realistic scene in our mind that makes sense of the speaker's words, we tend to add in details and background information that are not present in the speakers account.

We 'colour in' the speaker's account, and embellish upon what is said, adding in details so that we can imagine the scene that they are relaying to us.

We begin to imagine other details outside of the speaker's comment, what else is going on? What have they done? What are they going to do? How was this situation created? What will happen next?

And then we answer these questions for ourselves, so we find ourselves thinking, "I know where this is going, I know what they thinking, I know what's going to happen, I see how that happened, I know who gave them that idea, I know how they really feel about this, I can imagine how they said it to the other person," and so on.

We don't really know any of these things. We delude ourselves that we can 'mind read' and that somehow we know the extra meaning behind, and circumstances surrounding the speaker's comments.

This process of embellishing upon the speaker's account with our own judgements is 'mind reading' – thinking that you know what the speaker means, when really all you know is the meaning and representation that you have created in your mind, which will be different to the representation in the speaker's mind.

As you can imagine, by mind reading we are distorting the speaker's meaning so that we can make sense of it in our mind – so that it makes sense in, 'our world' and meets with 'our preconceptions'.

We have a natural tendency to mind read. It allows us to create a perceived reality around the speaker's words, and makes listening more enjoyable. When someone tells us a story we are encouraged to use our imagination. Novels would be a lot less enjoyable if we simply read the authors words without adding extra depth to our imagined pictures, sounds and feelings to make it seem real. Mind reading can be fun.

However; when you are listening, your mind reading can distort, and take you further away from, the speaker's intended meaning.

When the speaker is communicating an idea, opinion, plan or past event, the more you mind read, the further away you will be from sharing the same meaning of the words, or seeing their perspective, the more you will hear what you expected to hear and the less new information you will learn.

Investigative listening is about hearing what the speaker is really saying (rather than what you think they are saying), hearing what the speaker is omitting (rather than using your imagination to fill in the gaps) and knowing where to question to gain more precise information.

In order to listen accurately and take only the meaning that the speaker intends you must first STOP 'mind reading'.

Let's look at an example of mind reading in action. The first sentence below is delivered by the speaker. The four statements below are the meaning that the listener allocates to the speaker's comment.

Notice which ones are **presuppositions** – linguistic assumptions suggested by the specific words the speaker has used, and which are **mind reads** – additional information that is not really there in the speaker's sentence, the listener has added extra meaning.

So to clarify, a presupposition is assumed by the speaker – indicated by their choice of words, a mind read is stuff that you have made up.

Example 1

Speaker's words: **"I'm not sure if I will sell my car."**

Listener's interpretations: **The speaker has a car / The speaker likes their car / The speaker's car is for sale / The speaker thinks their car is rubbish.**

Let's look at each in turn:

The speaker has a car.
Presupposition – indicated by the words 'my car'.

The speaker likes their car.
Mind Read – nowhere in the speaker's sentence do they indicate whether they like their car or not.

The speaker's car is for sale.
Mind Read – there is no indication whether his car is currently for sale or not. Perhaps it is for sale and they are not sure if they will find a buyer, or maybe they are not sure if they will put the car on the market.

The speaker thinks their car is rubbish.
Mind Read – nowhere in the speaker's sentence do they indicate their opinion of the car.

118

Example 2

Speaker's words: **"I should stop shouting at my staff."**

Listener's interpretation: **The speaker has staff / The speaker is a bad boss / The speaker hates his staff / The speaker currently shouts at his staff.**

Again, taking each sentence in turn:

The speaker has staff.
Presupposition – indicated by the words 'my staff'.

The speaker is a bad boss.
Mind Read – how can we possibly know that? Bad in what way? There is no indication of how good or bad a boss the speaker is in the sentence.

The speaker hates their staff.
Mind Read – there is no indication of how the speaker feels about their staff.

The speaker currently shouts at their staff.
Presupposition – indicated by the word 'stop'. In order to stop shouting at their staff, that presupposes that they must currently be shouting at their staff.

Now it's your turn...

Mark the listener's interpretations as Presuppositions (P) or Mind Reads (MR):

1. *Speaker's Words:* **"I have to create unrealistic expectations."**

Listener's interpretation:

The speaker thinks they are a failure.

The speaker feels trapped.

The speaker has expectations.

The speaker knows their expectations are unrealistic.

2. *Speaker's Words:* **"The lack of communication was causing friction."**

Listener's interpretation:

The speaker is making people communicate.

There was a lack of communication in the past.

There was friction in the past.

Everyone is getting on well now.

3. *Speaker's Words:* **"If I don't learn these communication techniques, people will not do what I want."**

Listener's interpretation:

He feels powerless.

He doesn't know these communication techniques.

He wants to learn these communication techniques.

There are things that he wants people to do.

Interesting isn't it? How can you possibly listen impartially if you are adding content by filling in the gaps?

To investigate and accurately qualify what the speaker is attempting to communicate, you must first turn off your mind reads.

In general conversation, if you qualify everything this can become exhausting for the other person. We generally like to communicate at a very surface level.

As with all of these listening techniques, I would urge you to practise them and employ them only when you need more information than you are being provided.

There's a lot going on...

Right now, if someone to ask what you were doing you would probably saying "I'm reading". You may be slightly more specific and say, "I'm reading a book on NLP." And you would probably think that's an adequate description of your current activity.

Now take a moment to notice the many things that are omitted from that description. Are you standing, sitting or laying down? Is there anything else going on in the room, or are you outside, or on a train or plane? Are you hot or cold? Is it light or dark? Is it morning or afternoon?

Obviously, at any given moment there is a lot going on. In order for the volume of information involved in a human interaction to be effectively exchanged, we are required to summarise what we are describing. That's the only way to make it manageable and communicable.

If someone provides you with an account of what happened in a meeting that lasted half an hour, they may provide you with a five minute summary. In doing so, an enormous amount of information is missed out; the stuff that is considered less relevant by the speaker.

In addition, the speaker will be offering their interpretation of the meaning, their 'version' of events. They will be applying their values, beliefs, judgements and perceptions, and communicating the result of that process; rather than what actually happened. We all do this to some extent.

So how can you know when this is happening? How can you see what the speaker is distorting and hear what is being missed out. How can you notice the language patterns that indicate when the speaker is giving you a vague and ambiguous account?

If you feel that the speaker's account of things does not quite add up; how do you decide where to explore? How can you recognise the language that indicates the speaker is providing you with their 'version' and, what can you ask that will reveal the facts?

We will now go on to look at the Meta Model. This is the first NLP model coded by Bandler & Grinder as a result of modelling Fritz Pearls and Virginia Satir.

This powerful language model is extremely effective as it is based on syntactic patterning, and has successfully been implemented in many languages.

It (and its derivative models – the Precision Model, the Verbal Package) is the only model to date that effectively uses the syntactic patterns of grammar to become precisely specific and, by re-connecting the language with the reference experiences, allows the recovery of the deep structure of what's really going on.

In summarising information in order to make it communicable, the speaker does three things; they distort the information with their meanings and interpretations, they generalise about things, and they delete content that they consider to be irrelevant or taken for granted.

We will look at the Meta Model in three parts, breaking it down to address each of these three linguistic 'violations' in turn.

The Meta Model explicitly identifies the language patterns that indicate when the speaker is giving a 'surface level' account (Distorted, Deleted and Generalised), and explicitly how to challenge those language patterns to 'drill down' to the specifics of deeper structure.

If the previous paragraph was just a load of words that were difficult to attribute a meaning to that make them make sense, that's fine. I will go on to explain this process in more detail, breaking it down into more manageable chunks.

We know that the tendency to 'mind read' as a listener adds in a great deal of opportunity for misinterpretation, and by removing this tendency we are left with the details and assumptions provided by the speaker.

So what if the speaker's account does not make sense? What if you get the feeling they are not right somehow and can't see their error. How can you hear where they are providing you with their version of the facts, rather than just the facts? How do know when they have missed something out or biased the information with their 'model of the world'?

Would it be useful to be able to identify the patterns in their speech that indicate where and how they have biased the information they are relaying?

You can identify how a speaker biases information, providing you with their version or interpretation, which may well be different to yours if you were supplied with the original information.

In order to provide you with a feeling for how this works; let's start with an example paragraph of the type of statements that we hear in everyday summarised speech:

"This account makes me nervous. I know what they are thinking. If we are late for the meeting we will not get the deal. They left us waiting in reception; that means they are annoyed with us. This client is always looking for problems. We can't change their perception of us. The

problem is communication. The other supplier is better."

Would you agree that these are the patterns of language that we often hear? We tend to hear these words and nod in agreement or shrug our shoulders and say "maybe".

When you study the statements carefully you will notice that they are not facts. They are the speaker's interpretations of facts, generalised facts or there is so much missing that you have no idea what they are in fact about. Yet we seldom directly challenge the structure of the sentence.

In order to demonstrate this, let's look at each sentence in turn, and challenge it:

"This account makes me nervous."
Really? How does it do that? Are you sure it's not your perception of the account that makes you create the nervous feeling? What about this account makes you create the nervousness?

"I know what they are thinking."
How do you know? Have they told you? Do you have psychic abilities?

"If we are late for the meeting we will not get the deal."
How do you know that? Is that definite? Have you ever been late and got the deal?

"They left us waiting in reception; that means they are annoyed with us."
Does it? How do you know that? Could there be another reason? Are you sure they are not just running late?

"The client is always looking for problems."
Always? Are you sure about that? Every time? Constantly?

"We can't change their perception of us."
Are you sure? Can't? Maybe we haven't, but can't? Is there no possible way?

"The problem is communication."
What type of communication? Phone calls? Meetings? Emails? What about the communication is a problem?

"The other supplier is better."
Better than whom? Better at what? How are they better?

You can begin to see the many 'errors' that appear in summarised speech and get a feel for how they can be challenged.

We have the ability to intuitively challenge statements and presuppositions that are likely to be untrue, you simply need to put yourself in that mindset of evaluating what you hear, rather than allowing it to wash over you, or getting caught up in the subject matter so that the errors pass by unnoticed.

When you begin to listen to 'how' people are communicating rather than being caught up in 'what' they are communicating, you can precisely hear what they are presenting.

You can then begin to challenge the omissions in their speech (and possibly the omissions in their thinking) and drill down to uncover what's really going on.

It is clear that there are errors in these summarised statements, so how do these errors occur? How does summarising our thoughts 'mess up' our representation of a situation so much?

In summarising a situation to create a representation of a situation that we can reason from and effectively communicate, we do three things:

We distort the information by adding our meanings and interpretations.

We decide what something means; add an opinion or interpretation and decide what has happened, what will happen or what else is happening.

In doing this we are distorting information. We are taking a detail or an event, and distorting it by adding our interpretation or opinion.

We then communicate the result of that process rather than the original information.

For example:

"They left us waiting in reception; that means they are annoyed with us."

The speaker has taken the fact that they have been waiting in reception, and added the interpretation: that means they are annoyed with us.

It's a distortion, the speaker cannot possibly know this to be a fact, they are hallucinating it, creating it in their mind.

The second thing we do is we generalise by creating absolutes. We make judgements, rules and boundaries in our mind or exaggerate in quantifying things.

For example:

"The client is always looking for problems."

Is this likely to be true? Always? Perhaps it seems like that; perhaps they look for problems quite often, but always?

Generalisations are *never* true. ☺

...So neither is the sentence above. Generalising is a way of simplifying things in our mind. By ignoring the exceptions to the rule and making things absolute we are cutting down the variables to make an easier-to-manage representation in our mind.

As well as quantifying or qualifying things in an absolute way (as above) we also impose rules on things. The rules that we create in our mind and apply to our representation of things are indicated by Modal Operators. They are absolute and universally applied so they are also generalisations.

For example:

"We can't change their perception of us."

Really? It is not at all possible to do so? Maybe the speaker has not thought of how they can do this, but surely it's not impossible. 'Can't' is a definite universal rule. It's fairly obvious that 'can't' is usually not true. It is a boundary that the speaker is setting – the boundary does not really exist.

Try this out with any sentence you can think of with the word 'can't'. Is it really true? Or is it a choice that has been made into an impossibility in the speaker's mind?

The third thing we do is delete information. We just miss stuff out. We do not qualify what we are saying with fact, we just provide our conclusion.

For example:

"The other supplier is better."

The speaker is giving us the results of their appraisal. Their conclusion. It is not qualified in any way. There is no usable information in the sentence. Better at what? How are they better? What are we better at? And so on...

So, to reiterate: In summarising information to create a consciously manageable and communicable representation in their mind, the speaker does three things:

1. They distort the information by communicating their conscious representation of the information which will contain their meanings and interpretations.

2. They generalise and make 'rules' or 'boundaries' around their representation of the information to make it more absolute or black and white, thus easier to consciously deal with.

3. They delete information, communicating what they consciously consider to be the main points or the important bits, and miss out the original information that lead them to those conclusions, taking much of it 'as a given'.

Allow me to illustrate this with a more simplistic example in a different type of communication:

Consider the signs below which we instantly recognise as 'meaning' male and female:

I emphasize the word meaning because these are clearly not pictures or facsimile representations of a male and female; they are icons designed to effectively communicate the meaning male or female.

The purpose of this is not to communicate a human being of one sex or the other in explicit detail. The purpose is to provide a representation that will allow you to get the idea that is being communicated as quickly and easily as possible.

It is not relevant that every detail of the communication is technically correct as long as you get the meaning behind the communication.

In communicating at this level of efficiency we have clearly done three things:

We have distorted the image of a human: The heads are spherical, bodies and limbs are straight without curves and consistent in width from top to bottom, the female's dress is a perfect triangle.

We have deleted information: There are no facial features, no hands or feet, no hair or ears, no details at all within the outline.

We have generalised: both icons are the same height with the same shaped head and the same legs. The icon is a generalisation – do all women wear dresses?

The Meta Model provides us with the patterns that indicate when one of these three processes is taking place in our language, and how to challenge these Distortions, Deletions and Generalisations (DDG) in a way that provides you with more precise and detailed information.

I have retained the distinctions simply to make it easier to explain from my current frame of reference. However, I'm not interested in you being able to identify deletions, distortions and generalisations. I have met many people who explicitly know the Meta Model, but cannot hear the patterns when spoken in real time.

Instead I would like you to rely upon your innate and intuitive questioning ability. Just ask yourself instinctively; what's missing from the speaker's sentence? What's not qualified or ambiguous? What would you ask to qualify it?

Before we look at what you would say to challenge these DDGs, you will first need to become a bit more sensitive to them.

In the following exercise there are some sentences in which the speaker has missed details out, added their opinion or interpretation, or added universal rules and boundaries. With this in mind, read through them and make a note of what you notice. I would not expect you to be able to identify the errors in all of them yet – see how you get on:

"If we charge more then the client will go elsewhere."

_____

"This will never change."

_____

"They won't listen to you."

_____

"We have an issue with quality."

_____

"Deadlines make me stressed."

_____

"You arrived late, that means you don't care."

_____

"We need to make a change."

_____

"Everyone is upset about these changes."

_____

Why? Because...

Now have a go at challenging the deletions, distortions and generalisations.

On the next page is another list of sentences containing these three types of linguistic 'violation'. What question would you ask to get more detail from the speaker?

Put yourself in a bit of a 'doubting Thomas' mindset and challenge where you feel that what you see they are saying is incomplete. In creating questions to challenge these patterns, avoid asking 'why?'.

You may ask why not ask 'why?'; and the answer is because the answer to 'why?' is 'because...'.

When you ask 'why?', you are likely to get reasons rather than recovering any more specific information. The reasons will be surface level and full of Deletions, Distortions and Generalisations, just like the sentence that you are challenging. In other words, when you ask 'why?', you often get more of the same distorted, deleted and generalised stuff. (The exception to this is when people answer 'why?' by communicating intention or purpose).

Our intention in challenging Deletions, Distortions and Generalisations is to drill down beneath the surface structure information the speaker is providing making them more specific, thus removing the errors or violations in their sentence. Here's an example for the purpose of clarity:

The speaker says, **"This client is always angry."**

Assuming we know what client they are talking about, the questionable part of the sentence is the generalisation 'always'.

So what happens if we challenge the sentence, encouraging the speaker to be more specific:

Challenge: **Are they really 'always' angry or is it just often? OK, so when specifically are they angry?**

In the above example we are getting somewhere, we are beginning to get more specific information about this circumstance.

Let's look at the alternative:

Challenge: **Why are they angry?**

Because they don't like us, they don't want to work with us, they don't like their job. They have an attitude problem.

Asking why is getting us nowhere. We are still at that 'surface level'.

There are occasions when is it good to use the word 'why?'. However – when your intention is to gain more precise information from a speaker that is deleting, generalising and distorting the information, 'why' may not help you.

Now instinctively and intuitively challenge the sentences below, avoiding the question 'why?'.

As you make a note of your challenging question, think about what the speaker is forced to do in providing an answer. Imagine what the likely response to your challenge would be:

For example, on the previous page, the speaker was forced to question if the generalisation 'always' was true, and therefore be more specific about the circumstances around the client's anger.

"If we do not respond immediately the client will get annoyed."

"You don't understand what I'm saying."

"My boss did not stop and speak to me on the way to his office; that means he's angry with me."

"I need to see more commitment."

"They need to change their attitude."

"Sales targets make me feel under pressure."

By now you should be beginning to get an idea of how 'full of holes' our general speech is. I'm pretty sure that it was at about this point when I first began to ask, how do we manage to communicate anything at all?

Our everyday speech is so vague and full of ambiguity that it's amazing we are ever able to share an idea. Perhaps we don't really communicate our ideas as well as we think we do. Maybe we think we understand other people because we have been able to put a meaning on what they are saying that makes sense to us. That does not mean that it's what they intended to communicate.

We think we understand – but how can we know that our understanding is exactly the same as the speaker's understanding?

Now we are going to be explicit about the patterns of language that indicate when distortions, deletions or generalisations are happening, and demonstrate the most effective way to challenge the pattern to get below the surface structure and find out what's really going on.

1. The **first pattern** we will look at is particularly significant in the context of communication in the workplace. I don't know if you are familiar with the expression 'management speak'. If you are, there is a common function of this type of language:

Here are some examples of the pattern:

- "The problem is the communication in this office."
- "I need to see more commitment in the team."
- "There is no ownership."

The above sentences contain processes – communication, commitment, ownership.

These process words are being spoken about as if they are a thing. They have been made into a noun: For example: 'The communication'

What is 'the communication'? If it's a specific thing, what is it?

Is it phone calls? Meetings? E-mails? General conversations? Reporting systems? It will mean a different thing according to the context to which the listener is applying the word.

Communication is not a specific thing; it's a process that has been frozen in time to become treated as a noun.

This is an example of a **NOMINALIZATION**.

I need to see more *'commitment'*, there is no *'ownership'*. What do these words mean? There is not only one specific meaning that can be applied to these words.

I'm sure that the speaker knows what the word means when they use it, but the word is insufficient to communicate that specific, contextual meaning.

Imagine if I were to say, "You need to work on your communication." You may take from that that I would like you to be up-to-date with your written correspondence. I could mean that you need to speak up more in meetings (or any one of a hundred other interpretations of the word).

How do you challenge a nominalization? Turn it back into a verb to recover the process:

"The problem is the **communication** in this office."
How are we not communicating?
How would you like us to communicate?

"I need to see more **commitment** in the team."
How would we show more commitment?
How are we not showing commitment?

Your turn. Provide a challenge or two for **"There is no ownership."**

_____

_____

2. Below are some examples of the **second pattern**:

   - "I know what you are thinking about this."
   - "I see why you did that."
   - "I know what your intentions are."
   - "How can they possibly know?"

I know you are thinking about when you have heard people say things similar to or the same as the sentences above. Hang on, how can I possibly know that?

This pattern is a **MIND READ.**

The speaker is claiming to know what is going on inside someone else. How can they possibly know?

You experienced turning off your own mind reads earlier. Now you can begin to spot them when communicated by other people.

To challenge a MIND READ, simply question the source of the information – how they know what they claim to know:

"I know what you are thinking about this."
   How do you know?

"I see why you did that."
   How can you see my reasons?

"I know what this is really about."
   How do you know?

Your turn. Provide a challenge to **"I know what your intentions are"**.

_____

3. The **third pattern** is indicated by cause-effect thinking as per the examples below:

- "This account makes me nervous."
- "My boss makes me get angry."
- "Sales targets make me feel under pressure."
- "Deadlines make me stressed."

What is it about the account that you respond to by making yourself nervous?

Is it your boss that makes you angry, or is it your inflexible reaction to something that your boss does that creates the anger?

To challenge **CAUSE-EFFECT**, ask about the process, how it happens:

"This account **makes me** nervous."
How do you choose to feel nervous when working with this account?
How does this account cause you to make yourself nervous?

"My boss **makes me** get angry."
How do you choose to get angry about your boss?
How does you boss cause you to make yourself angry?

"**If** we are late **then** we will lose the business."
How do you know? Have you ever been late and got the business?

Your turn. Challenge **"Deadlines make me stressed"**.

---

4. The **fourth pattern**:

- "They left us waiting in reception; that means they are annoyed with us."
- "The new system means more pressure."
- "My boss did not stop and speak to me on the way to his office; that means he's angry with me."
- "You arrived late, that means you don't care."

Look at what the speaker has done here:

They have taken an experience ("They left us waiting in reception"), and added on an interpretation ("**that means** they are annoyed with us").

As if the two things are synonymous.

"My boss did not stop and speak to me on the way to his office" – well that's a factual experience...

"**That means** he's angry with me" – does it? How on earth could you be sure of that? How many other explanations could there be?

This pattern is a **COMPLEX EQUIVALENCE**

The speaker has done an equation in their head and made the external experience = their internal process.

For example: New system = more pressure.

To challenge a complex equivalence, challenge the equation:

"They left us waiting in reception; that **means** they are annoyed with us."
> **How does us waiting mean they are annoyed? Are you sure?**
> **Have you ever been kept waiting by someone who was not annoyed?**

"The new system **means** more pressure."
> **How are you equating the new system with pressure?**

"You arrived late, that **means** you don't care."
> **How does their late arrival indicate how much they care?**
> **Have you ever arrived late when you did care?**

Your turn. "**My boss did not stop and speak to me on the way to his office; that means he's angry with me.**"

---

5. You can also challenge other **PRESUPPOSITIONS** made by the speaker (the **fifth pattern**).

There will be a more explicit explanation of presuppositions in the speaking section. For now rely upon your ability to identify what the speaker has assumed in order for their sentence to make sense. Below is a list of presuppositions with an indication of what is being presupposed. You can challenge any presupposition by challenging how the speaker has arrived at that assumption.

"When will you **stop** worrying about small details?"
How do you assume I am currently worrying about small details?

"Have you read this **fascinating** book?"
How have you decided that the book is fascinating?

"Will you do the report now **or** later?"
What makes you think I will be doing the report?

Get the idea? See what I'm doing? Can you hear what the speaker is doing? Challenge the presupposition by challenging how they are assuming that this is true.

Your turn. **"Are you finding this easy *yet*?"**
What is this sentence assuming; how would you challenge it?

---

6. The **sixth pattern is UNIVERSAL QUANTIFIERS.** It's the patterns of speech that you usually easily recognise as generalisations:

- "This client is **always** looking for problems."
- "These things will **never** change."
- "He will get it wrong **every time**."
- **"Everyone** is upset about these changes."

These generalisations are seldom really true.

It is much easier for you to make things universal in your mind, rather than being constantly aware of the small number of exceptions to the rule. There are usually exceptions to these universal quantifiers.

The way to challenge a generalisation is to challenge the generalisation. So in the case of a universal quantifier, challenge the universal quantifier:

"This client is **always** looking for problems."
Always?

"These things will **never** change."
Never? Never ever???

135

"He will get it wrong **every time.**"
Every Time? Can you think of a time when he got it right?

Your turn. **"Everyone is upset about these changes."**

---

7. The **seventh pattern** is the rules and boundaries that we impose upon our world.

Think about it; when you say, *"I won't"* you are creating a rule in your mind. This rule is absolute. It is generalised, it is not taking into account any exceptions to that rule.

These rules are **MODAL OPERATORS** of positive/negative possibility or positive/negative necessity.

Again, as with all generalisations, modal operators are not really universally true. For example:

"I can't go out tonight."

Really? Can't? It is absolutely impossible is it?

Unless you are in prison, the chances are that this modal operator of negative possibility is not really true.

You can go out, and you are choosing not to for whatever reason. It could be that there are consequences in going out, or there is something more important to do instead. Either way it's a choice. It is possible to go out, you are just choosing otherwise. The choice has been removed as you make the decision to stay in into a rule. It's easier to think in absolutes. You say (and think), "I can't."

The way to challenge a modal operator is to challenge the modal operator itself:

"We can't change their perception of us."
We can't? Surely there are many ways of changing perception? What prevents us? What would happen if we did?

"They won't listen to you."
They won't? No matter what I do?

"You mustn't let them know your intentions."
Mustn't? What would happen if we did?

Your turn. **"We must get this deal. We have to change this immediately."**

---

8. The **eighth pattern** is a **LOST PERFORMATIVE.**

It's a value judgement: good/bad/right/wrong/positive/negative, etc. For example: "Learning NLP is a good thing."

You can see how that sentence has generalised about the whole NLP model, describing is as, generally, overall, a good thing.

We have no idea what this judgement is based upon or who is making the judgement. To challenge a value judgement you can challenge the judgement itself by challenging it directly or challenging where it came from.

For example:

"It's bad to be disorganised."
Who says? How is it bad?

"Regular meetings are a good thing."
Who says? What is good about them?

"It's important that you contribute."
Who says? How is it important?

Your turn. **"The meeting was positive. The atmosphere is in the office is negative."**

---

9. The **ninth pattern** is a **SIMPLE DELETION.**

This occurs when the speaker provides you with a perception or conclusion and no information to qualify it.

For example:

"I'm stressed."

This statement provides us with no specific information.

I'm sure that you can think of several questions that you would instinctively ask this person – **"What are you stressed about? What's happening that has caused you to make yourself stressed?"**

To challenge a simple deletion, ask what has been deleted.
More examples:

"I'm late."
What are you late for?

"They're worried."
What are they worried about?

Your turn. **"I'm annoyed. They are unhappy."**

---

10. We also often draw comparisons (the **tenth pattern**). A **COMPARATIVE DELETION** is where the speaker uses comparative words, without being specific about what the subject of the sentence is compared to...

To be more explicit, an example of this would be saying something is better, without specifying what it is better than:

"The new system is **better**."
Better than what? Better than the old system? Better than another system? Better than expected?

A comparative deletion is indicated by comparative words: Better, best, worst, more, less, most, least, superior, inferior, quicker, slower etc.

A comparative deletion is challenged by challenging what the comparison is made against.

"Delivery is quite **slow**."
Slow compared to what?

"It is of the highest quality."
Compared to what?

"Your service is **expensive**."
Expensive compared to what?

Your turn. **"Our competitors' service is better. These communication techniques are an improvement."**

---

11. A LACK OF REFERENTIAL INDEX fails to specify the 'who' or 'what' that the sentence is referring to (the **eleventh pattern**):
For example:

"They won't listen."
Who are they?

To challenge a lack of referential index, ask for clarification of the missing 'who' or 'what'. For example:

"People usually make these mistakes."
Who make these mistakes? What people? What mistakes?

"The computers have developed a problem."
What computers specifically? What problem?

Your turn. **"He lost his temper in the office yesterday. We need to have a meeting about this project."**

To summarise the Meta model, the previous patterns indicate precisely where, in their constructing of a sentence, the speaker has biased or missed out information.

The questioning techniques will recover the process behind any biased information and specify any unqualified information.

The next time you are provided with information that is vague and summarised to the point where you are not gaining the level of understanding you require, you can question with precision using these techniques.

There are several types of question that you could ask for all of the violations listed in the Meta Model. In addition, the patters seldom appear in isolation; any given sentence can contain several of these Meta Violations.

Rather than clearly dividing the model into distortions, deletion and generalisations, and specifying which is which, I have lumped it together. It is not important to identify the process using these descriptions. It is important that become sensitive to hearing ambiguity in the speakers account of things.

You may notice that I have limited the questions I have used for the purpose of simplicity so they fall into three distinct types of question:

When the speaker has added their interpretation or opinion and distorted the information in the process I have challenged **HOW** the person has arrived at this conclusion.

For generalisations and absolute thinking like universal quantifiers and the rules or boundaries indicated by modal operators and lost performatives; I have challenged **THE GENERALISATION** itself.

For all the deleted patterns where there is information that's unqualified or missing I have challenged **WHAT** has been deleted.

This should provide you with a 'rule of thumb' that simplifies the Meta Model questioning.

The most important thing is that you develop an awareness of when the speaker is biasing or missing out information so that you can instinctively challenge them.

The question you ask is not so important, as long as you are removing the Distortions, Deletions and Generalisations in the speaker's account – provoking them to be more specific.

Another way of unpacking it...

One of the developments of New Code NLP is the introduction of the Verbal Package.

It is a simplified version of the Meta Model, as it achieves the same result of drilling down to specifics simply by specifying the unspecified verbs and nouns, and adding a provocative paraphrase.

I would like to cover the first part of this technique briefly:

When provided with a vague and summarised sentence, you can gain more specificity by challenging 'how' the speaker does the unspecified verbs and exactly 'what' unspecified nouns are. For example:

"I went to see a client."

The unspecified **noun** is 'the client' so you would ask, "Which client?"
Answer: "Acme Corp."
To specify the noun further: "Which contact at Acme Corp?"
Answer: "John Smith."

The unspecified **verb** is 'went' (to go), so the verb specifying question would be, "How did you get there?"

Answer: "On the train."

You now have a new noun that you can challenge: "Which train?"

Answer: "The train from X to destination Y."

So we have gone from:

"I went to see a client"

to:

"I travelled on the train from X to Y to see John Smith at Acme Corp."

It's a very easy way to uncover more precise and detailed information.

If you are interested in practising this part of the pattern, I suggest that you pick some of the examples of vague and summarised sentences form the Meta Model section and experiment with what would happen if you simply qualified the unspecified nouns and verbs.

The second part of this pattern, the provocative paraphrase, I would like to cover in more detail:

The Farrelly Model

Before being explicit about the second part of the Verbal Package – the provocative paraphrase, I would like to share with you how it was coded and quote the following from *Whispering in the Wind* (Bostic/Grinder, 2001):

> *On the occasion of being invited to be keynote speakers at a Frontiers of Psychiatry forum sponsored by Temple University in Philadelphia in the late 70's, Grinder and Bandler leveraged the opportunity by proposing to the forum director that he invite Frank Farrelly to work with an actual client on stage in front of the 300 psychiatrists attending the conference. The agreement was that immediately succeeding Farrelly's work, Bandler and Grinder would present an explicit representation of the key portions of what he had done – that is, they would model Frank's behaviour, making his patterning explicit. Bandler and Grinder were already familiar with Farrelly's verbal patterning through his highly instructive, as well as amusing, book Provocative Therapy, and they had strong*

suspicions that they would find as well a number of non-verbal behaviours of excellence in his performance that they had already coded from their earlier research.

Frank's demonstration was superb – to give a flavour of his verbal work as well as offer the reader an example of his hallucinatory strategy for specifying language, we reproduce several exchanges between Farrelly and his client.

After a couple of minutes of relatively content free chatting between the two men (and during which it was clear, Frank was capturing the full conscious as well as unconscious attention of this client – typically referred to as rapport – primarily using the mirroring strategy coded in NLP), the following exchange occurred:

Frank: "OK, well, what do you want me to do for you?"

Client: "Well, the thing that is bothering me is, well, my relationship with my wife."

Frank: "Oh yeah, I know what you mean – limited sexual positions in bed."

Client: (after a puzzled pause)" No, I mean I just don't feel as close to her as I used to."

Frank: OK, I got it – the two of you are just not 'getting it on' as you used to.

Client: (again, a pause) "No, that's not it – it's that we simply don't seem to talk about things together any more."

Frank: "So you don't talk about new ways to make it together."

Client: (again, a pause) "No, I mean that we don't talk about the way we are raising the kids, or what we are going to do when we retire... (continuing to enumerate the specifics of what they don't talk about)."

A narrative representation of Farrelly's strategy would be to simply: get connected then select any important noun or verb offered by the client – some vague term that indicates a very large set of possibilities in the world that the client could be referring to. From this set, select any highly specific and provocative interpretation that you suspect is absolutely off the mark and present it congruently to the client as if you actually believe it. Listen to the response and repeat the cycle until you achieve the specificity that you desire.

142

The first time I became aware of this pattern it was being demonstrated to me (and forty or so other people) by John Grinder.

I found it interesting, very entertaining, and, having not yet experienced the pattern in real scenarios, was unaware of the subtle, agreeable and powerful nature of the pattern.

In fact, the reason that I have included the Verbal Package in this book is because of how simple and empowering the use of paraphrasing is in business.

In applying this pattern to business I discovered two things:

1. That this pattern works very effectively as a 'stand alone' technique – you can get terrific results without first asking Meta Model or Noun/Verb specifying questions.
2. That it works without the deliberate misunderstanding – even when you genuinely attempt to understand the technique is just as effective; it exposes our genuine misunderstandings.

There is little point in me stressing how invisible this technique is. If you congruently provide the appearance of genuinely attempting to understand, the person with whom you are using the pattern will not be paying much attention to what *you* said, they will be paying attention to what *they* have not said.

I am also not going to go into detail about how compelled people will be to explain themselves further when they think that their previous communication has been misunderstood.

I suggest that you experiment with the pattern yourselves and prepare to be amazed by the results. There are two ways that I would invite you to practise this pattern:

Firstly, to gain an understanding of how much you can 'get away with', practise the pattern in a social environment where there is a good level of natural rapport.

In doing so, demonstrate an eagerness to really understand the other person and be as outrageous as you can with deliberate misunderstandings, then watch what people say back to you. It's the best way to get a feel for how the pattern works. Entertain yourself as much as possible with this game.

Now let's put this into a business context:

In the workplace, some people have expressed a reluctance to deliberately misunderstand other people, especially people more senior to them in their organisation.

In order to overcome this, I began to think of how to make the pattern easier to use. My intention was to do whatever it takes so that the individual becomes comfortable using the technique, and I would hope that this would lead to more behavioural flexibility in the future.

In 'softening' this pattern I discovered that it is almost as effective without the deliberate misunderstanding. It works as follows:

Take the speaker's statement and feed it back 'framed' with the intention to confirm understanding – adding in a detail where they have been vague or ambiguous:

- **Possible outcome 1.** The speaker will agree: You have been conscientious, valued whatever they are saying by taking the trouble to confirm that you understand and communicated your understanding. This often helps to build more rapport.

- **Possible outcome 2.** They will not agree and it will compel them to be more specific, providing you with a clearer indication of what their point really is. A potential misunderstanding has been eliminated.

Example 1:

A: "This new process will not work."
B: "Just so that I understand; what you are telling me is that this new process will take longer."
A: "No; I'm saying that it will not record information that we need."
B: "Oh, I see, you are concerned about compliance."
A: "No; we are missing out on vital CRM data."

Example 2:

A: "We have a delivery problem with this project."
B: "Just so that I understand; what you are telling me is that we will be late."
A: "Yes – exactly – by about 4 days."

In both cases, the pattern is providing us with specific information.

Before we conclude this section, a brief word of caution:

The barriers and boundaries in peoples' speech can indicate the barriers and boundaries in their thinking.

My experience is that the reason their language is deleted, distorted and generalised is because their current frame of reference is deleted, distorted and generalised.

We mentioned earlier that language is the 'software' of the brain. We use our 'linguistic map' for our deductive thinking process.

When you challenge the surface structure of language, you are often challenging the person's model of the world – so handle with care.

Some people have a very rigid model of the world and to 'break it up' can be a very emotive process.

Only use Meta Model questions, the verbal package or indeed any NLP technique when you are in rapport with the person you are questioning, otherwise you may get a variety of unwanted results.

If you 'drill down' using several of these patterns in succession you will either break rapport or end up with the other person fully associated into what is currently limiting their flexibility. Not ideal for dinner parties.

Summing up

- Words mean different things to different people; words are unreliable.
- As a listener, we tend to 'mind read', hallucinating additional meaning that is not provided in the speakers account.
- In 'summarising' information and creating their representation or 'model of the world' the speaker has distorted information – biasing it with their interpretation, generalised – making things absolute and setting boundaries, and deleted information – missing bits out, being vague and ambiguous.
- You can use the Meta Model to effectively challenge distortions, deletions and generalisations, and recover what's going on underneath the surface structure. The patterns detailed in the Meta Model are:

> Nominalization, Mind Read, Cause-Effect,
> Complex Equivalence, Any Incorrect
> Presupposition, Universal Quantifiers, Modal

Operators, Lost Performative, Simple Deletions, Comparative Deletions, Lack of Referential Index.

- The verbal package is a simplified model to challenge vague and ambiguous speech and includes paraphrasing which can be very powerful in the workplace.

5. Influential Speaking

'Framing' and the Milton Model

What is influential speaking?

Some years ago I attended a business event where I watched and listened to speeches from two speakers.

The first speaker strode confidently on to the stage. He was immaculately dressed, well groomed and I thought 'this guy means business'. He went on to deliver a very professional and informative speech – well presented and full of interesting facts using clear and attractive looking slides. At the end of this speech there were no questions.

I thought it was a hard act to follow as the second speaker took the stage. He walked on casually and was not armed with well prepared slides. There didn't seem to be much structure, he began speaking by asking the audience a question. After a few seconds I realised that I was engrossed. It was as if he was talking to me, I could personally relate to everything that he said. I was very impressed by the first speaker, and this one was far more interesting, and he was the kind of person that I would 'get along with'. I felt like I was getting to know him. At the end there were a variety of enthusiastic questions, and he clearly seemed to enjoy answering every one of them, making more of a connection with every person that he answered.

I wondered what the second speaker was doing that the first was not. Here were two men doing essentially the same thing, and yet they were getting completely different responses. The first speech was clear and interesting, the second was somehow more of an experience, although I couldn't really say what was different. There must have been a difference in what they were doing or how they were doing it. Was this something you can learn? If so I wanted to learn it. But surely this communication style is something you are born with, how can I learn it if I can't even define it? That was, of course, before I had heard of NLP.

Before we begin this section I would like to be explicit about what I mean by influence:

In my world, influence is communicating an idea to someone in such a way that they want to do as you ask and they are motivated to do so.

If someone does something because they are 'told to' or because they fear the consequences of not doing so this is not influential communication – it's delivering orders or 'pulling rank'.

I would like to ask you the following provocative questions:

- Is someone motivated by your reasons or theirs?
- Do they agree because they simply accept that you must be right, or because they can actually see your point of view?
- Can people best relate to your experiences or their own?
- What is influence? What needs to be present as a dynamic for influence to exist; what dynamic makes people resistant?

Think about it for a minute...

To pre-frame this chapter

Have you ever found yourself saying, "No, no, that's not what I meant." And wishing you could start again?

We will be covering the topic of 'speaking' in two sections:

Firstly, how to 'frame' language to manage the other person's experience.

Just think for a moment about communications in the past that have been unproductive or broken down. Maybe you have had meetings or interactions that did not reach a positive outcome. Consider the dynamics of these conversations.

To make this point explicitly, if there is no agreement, there can be no influence. I think it would be helpful for you to think of it in the following simplistic terms: Agreement is influence – disagreement is resistance.

Think about it for a moment; the people who you find influential, do you also find them agreeable?

Think of the people who you fundamentally disagree with; how influenced are you by them?

You can prime the interaction within an agreed frame – managing the other person's expectation and attention direction, make your comments more agreeable, maintain agreement regardless of how the other person responds and keep everything 'on track'.

This workbook covers how these 'frames' can be used practically and easily.

Secondly, how to guide the listeners experience using influential language patterns – The Milton Model.

This is the language of 'Ericksonian' hypnosis – coded by Richard Bandler and John Grinder in modelling Milton Erickson.

We will be covering how you can use many of these permissive and persuasive language patterns in the context of business.

You can create agreement by structuring your language in such a way that it is difficult to disagree; and add influence by guiding the listeners' experience and providing agreeable suggestions.

Framing your communication

1. Pre-frame

The previous page was a 'pre-frame' for this chapter. So what was the point of doing that?

Imagine, for a moment being called into a meeting with no idea what the meeting is about. Your mind will be racing, attempting to attribute meaning to the interaction. At the first ambiguous communication you will begin to 'mind read'; jumping to (often incorrect) conclusions.

The person who has called the meeting can have little influence over you, and the interaction is unlikely to become agreeable and cooperative, until you have that understanding of why you are there, what it's about or how it is likely to proceed.

If you want the undivided attention of the listener, pre-frame the communication.

If for any reason your pre-frame meets with resistance, this will highlight a lack of agreement at the most fundamental level. If the purpose and parameters of the communication are not agreed then what's the point of starting the meeting? You will be 'talking at crossed purposes', you will not see eye-to-eye, and afterwards you may feel that you had attended different meetings.

When you pre-frame the communication and the pre-frame is accepted, you are beginning at a point of agreement. You have also 'primed' the thinking of the listener, moving their attention to whatever the topic is, and you have defined what is relevant.

Until you have arrived at an agreement about what the meeting is about, you may be presented with a lot of irrelevant information, and it's difficult to challenge the relevancy of that information unless you have set a frame around what is (and therefore what is not) relevant. How do you know what's relevant and irrelevant if there is not an explicit framing of the parameters and intentions of the meeting?

Here's an NLP 'Big Idea' that is particularly relevant:

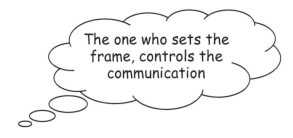

The one who sets the frame, controls the communication

Any experience that you have will be primed with a frame. Generally speaking there will be some kind of purpose or expectation for any action. Those purposes and expectations will frame the experience governing your attention direction – paying attention to that which is relevant to that purpose, excluding from your awareness that which is not.

Imagine arriving slightly late at a busy train station. You need to purchase a ticket and find your train in a hurry. These intentions will 'frame' your experience. You will become aware of the things that relate to purchasing tickets and boarding a train – signs, ticket machines, ticket booths, departure information, platform numbers, the sound of the announcer's voice over a loudspeaker, etc.

You are likely to be oblivious to newspaper vendors or anything else happening in the train station that is not relevant to your purpose. They will escape your attention (unless they are surprising or unusual).

Your experience has been framed, and your awareness is focused on what falls within that frame.

We constantly create frames of reference that allow us to allocate meaning to experiences and communication. Without a current frame of reference we have no idea 'what to make of' those experiences or communications.

For example, as you work your way through this book, you are aware that it is about business communication, so you will have a frame of reference that you apply these words to, whether they be past interactions with people, imagined future interactions or just the words that you say in your own head. Either way you are unlikely to be thinking of where you went to school, the last film you watched at the cinema or Elvis Presley (until I mention them of course).

Let's move back to the practical application of this idea; the pre-frame.

Imagine if someone were to call you into a meeting and start by saying, "We need to look at your performance."

How would you feel? What would you be thinking?

In the absence of a reason or intention for the meeting your mind will be leaping to conclusions in order to create a 'frame' of reference for what is about to follow. When a frame for an interaction is not provided you will create one; and the frame you create could easily be unhelpful or different to the speaker's intention for the meeting.

Now imagine the difference if the meeting was pre-framed with: "We are putting a quarterly performance appraisal in place to serve as a milestone indicator at the end of the year and I would value your input in completing your appraisal form. It should take about 5 minutes, nothing will happen immediately as a result unless an important issue is raised."

Does that feel different?

You now know what the meeting is about, the intention and reason behind it and what you are expected to do. You can divert your attention to the things that are relevant within this 'frame'.

Some more examples of pre-frames to prime the listener would be:

"The purpose of this meeting is......"

"Today, I would really like for us to concentrate on......"

"My intention in calling this meeting is......"[*]

You can also utilise an effective pre-frame if a meeting goes 'off track'. Having created a frame of reference, you can challenge the relevancy of things that fall outside of that frame, and bring things back on track by reminding participants of reasons, intentions and desired outcomes. For example:

---

[*] The last example of a pre-frame is particularly useful. If you do not make your positive intention explicit, the listener may 'mind read' your intention and get it very wrong. They could easily tell themselves that your intention is negative. Sharing intentions and communicating at the level of intention is extremely powerful as it separates your intent from the content of the communication. Assuming that your intention is positive, if you make the other person explicitly aware of your positive intention it makes it impossible for them to 'shoot the messenger' whatever the message.

"Remember that what we really need to see from this meeting is..."

"OK, we are aware of the problem, we agreed the intention of this meeting is to find a solution..."

It's not possible to bring people's attention back to within a particular frame of reference if that frame has not already been set and agreed upon.

2. Softening

I often travel into London on the train and on these occasions have a pleasant routine. I drive to the nearest train station, a small Victorian building in rural Hampshire, park my car, then purchase my train ticket and a car parking ticket from the ticket office.

One particular recent morning I arrived at the car park and found the ticket office to be closed. For a moment, my mind went blank with that type of confusion you get when something unexpected interrupts your routine.

I realised the large orange object near to my car was a car parking ticket machine so I scraped together all of the change I could find, even the coins under the drivers seat of my car, and approached the machine.

I found myself fifty pence short of the required amount. I considered driving to the nearest place that could provide me with change, and that would mean missing my train and arriving late at my appointment. I considered leaving my car without a ticket and then noticed a sign that indicated substantial fines enforced by wheel clamping.

I decided to rely upon the kindness of strangers. I approached the nearest person, a tall, well-presented man, and said, "Excuse me, I don't know if you have ever been in this situation before, and I'm very embarrassed, I need to get on the next train and I do not have enough change to buy a car parking ticket. I usually buy it from the ticket office (gesturing towards the locked building). I was wondering if you can lend me fifty pence. I know what you are thinking; I may not see you again so I suppose I'm asking you to give me fifty pence, and you can feel generous that you are helping me out enormously."

The man smiled warmly, nodded, agreed and kindly gave me the fifty pence I required.

A few moments later I was sitting on the train reflecting about what had happened and I thought: I wonder what would have happened if I had just said, "Please can you give me fifty pence."

I may well have had a different outcome.

We instinctively know, from an early age, that when we want something from someone, it helps if we soften the request. Then we enter the workplace where we are surrounded with processes and defined responsibilities, and we become very 'matter of fact' about our requests and seldom take the time to soften them.

What is the consequence of this? Neglecting to soften your requests may be quicker or more efficient, and it does little to motivate the other person, to win them over to being 'on your side'.

They may take offence to requests that are not softened, or they may become defensive, perceiving the request or instruction as an attack. In these conditions you can not influence or motivate the other person. They may well do what you ask, and if they are not motivated, how much effort will they put in? How much do they care about the result? What is this doing to your long-term working relationship?

Allow me to illustrate how this works in everyday situations:

You are in the workplace and you want to know if someone has finished a report that they were working on.

Scenario A:

You walk up to them and say, "Have you finished that report?"

What *meaning* are they likely to put on that interaction? Maybe something like: you expect it to be finished by now; you need it urgently; you think they have been distracted or talking too much.

There could be a huge variety of 'mind reads' going on (nearly all of which are likely to be wrong of course, but you have still created an opportunity for these incorrect mind reads to happen).

How is the other person likely to respond having perceived the interaction in a confrontational way?

How forthcoming will they be in providing information or explaining any difficulties if they are answering defensively?

Scenario B:

Instead of efficiently, abruptly and directly asking the question, you could say, "I'm just wondering; have you finished that report?"

The meaning the listener will put on this will be completely different. Because you are just wondering, whatever their answer is, that's OK.

The listener's behaviour is far more likely to be open and cooperative. If the answer they give is a problem for you (for example – the report is late and you do need it now) you have maintained a positive and open dialogue, so it is far easier to become aware of the real reasons and motivate the person to help you find a solution for the problem.

Softening your requests and instructions will provide positive results in gaining cooperation and maintaining an agreeable atmosphere.

More importantly in the context of influential speaking, it is very important to master this technique if you wish to become more influential. Softening allows you to deliver COMMANDS to the listener without them noticing the nature of the command – the listener will hear it as a soft question and respond it as a direct command without resistance (assuming a good level of rapport). You can use softening to say things that you would never 'get away with' if the sentence were not softened.

You will need to master the soft delivery of commands to effectively utilise the powerful patterns of the Milton Model.

Here are some examples. The command or confrontational statement within the softened statement is underlined:

"I'm just wondering if you can <u>do that for me now</u>."

"It's interesting if you <u>pay attention to this now</u>, you can..."

"I don't know when you will <u>notice that this is very important</u>."

"I'm not sure if <u>you can do this immediately</u>."

When considering the consequences of delivering comments, instructions or requests without softening them, it brings me to another 'Big Idea':

It is simply not possible to 'not communicate'. If you do nothing, people will attribute a meaning to it.

Besides which, it's impossible to do nothing – you are constantly communicating non-verbally. It is impossible to abstain, your body language will be talking even if you are not, and the interpretations of this communication will often be varied and inaccurate.

If you accept that you are always communicating, it makes it difficult to hide behind a 'matter of fact' approach. You may think that you are simply asking questions about and relaying facts, and there will be another level of communication happening whether you intend for it to happen or not.

If you accept that the communication process is happening at all times, you may as well do what you can to manage it and get the results that you want.

3. Maintaining agreement

Before I provide an explicit definition of this frame, I would like you to imagine a scenario:

Imagine the scene: You are in a meeting with someone and you volunteer an opinion on a particular subject. At that moment in time, your opinion is your opinion, so in your world it's right, or at the very least, valid. It is how you feel about this subject so your opinion deserves to be recognised.

The other person in the meeting, having constructed their reply before you finished speaking, immediately says, "No, you are wrong." In a very definite way, and then begins to give you their viewpoint.

What happens at the moment they immediately and abruptly dismiss your opinion?

How do you feel about your point being ignored? How do you react to your opinion being immediately rejected? What's your first thought when the quality of your input is challenged in this way?

I don't know what your answers to the above would be, and I'm sure that you have noticed that this abrupt and dismissive 'no' has a negative effect on the dynamics of the conversation.

Perhaps you would think 'he didn't listen to me'. Maybe you would immediately go inside and re-evaluate your opinion, or defend your opinion by constructing your counter-argument – 'no, I am right because........'

Either way, you and the other person are no longer communicating in an agreeable way. You have almost stopped listening to them, distracted by your own internal dialogue, and you will certainly not be convinced by their point.

Now 'put the boot on the other foot...'

Imagine that someone is speaking to you, they volunteer an opinion and you say, "No".

Maybe they are completely wrong in your opinion; but what have you achieved by dismissing their opinion abruptly? What have you done to the dynamics of the interaction? Will you be unable to influence them, or demonstrate how you think they are wrong in a way that they will accept if they are reacting to the "No"?

In order to speak influentially, there is one 'Big Idea' that is an essential operating principle:

Respect each person's model of the world

By now I would imagine that you are beginning to accept that the map is not the territory and that we all live in different worlds.

I don't know what you think about the sandwich spread Marmite. My business partner Ben and I disagree about this frequently.

I love it, it has a taste like nothing else, it's really strong and sort of spicy, it has loads of flavour and it's great on a bit of toast.

Ben hates it, he says, "It's odious – straight from the devil's pantry". There are strict rules in his house about a knife that has come into contact with Marmite going anywhere near the butter dish.

Do you think either one of us will be able to convince the other that they are wrong?

The reason for this is simple: In his world, he is right; in my world, I am right; and we both live in different worlds.

When someone speaks, whether they are correct or incorrect, in their world they are right.

When communicating and influencing, we are concerned only with the results we get; where we arrive at rather than where we start from.

If you were to give someone directions for how to walk or drive somewhere, you would not simply provide an accurate description of the destination.

You would need to start from where they are right now, and then describe the next road, and then the next road.

You need to start from where they are right now, because, that's where they are. Simply telling them that they are on the wrong road will not help them. You need to utilise the road they are on right now, rightly or wrongly, and provide guidance that will allow them to use different roads with the intention of moving them closer to the destination that is right for them.

Back to the practical pattern that will allow you to avoid disagreement – The agreement frame.

This pattern is so powerful it's like a linguistic martial art. I regularly practise karate and if someone were to come flying toward me with a punch or a kick, which happens regularly, the last thing I would do is attempt to stop their attack. I simply get out of the way; I guide the energy of their attack past me with as little resistance on my part as possible.

Consider the difference between the following two interactions:

Example 1:

Speakers statement: "This book is too difficult."
Response: "No it's not."
Speaker: "Yes it is, I'm telling you that I'm finding it difficult."
Response: "You just need to practise."
Speaker: "That doesn't help me right now."

Example 2:

Speakers statement: "This book is too difficult."
Response: "**That's right,** and it's interesting how new things always become easier with practice."

By first agreeing with the speaker, you negate the 'yes it is – no it isn't' pantomime.

You can then influence the speaker by making a statement that is agreeable.

(Note: to ensure that the statement you make is agreeable and relevant, chunk it up to a higher logical level of which their presenting statement is a member of that set. The easiest way to do this quickly is to 'mind read' the positive intention behind their original statement. If you are

thinking, "What?" – I do not expect you to understand what is written in this paragraph on your first read through this workbook. However, we will cover logical levels in the chapter on Negotiation, so just in case you refer to this book again in the future, it's helpful to have this tip.)

To make this pattern functional, simply acknowledge the speaker's statement positively so that they are comfortable before going on to add information or perspective that may contradict their original statement:

For example:

"That's right; I thought the same at first and when you take into account some other factors you will probably change your mind..."

"Yes; and perhaps a better way of achieving the same intention could be..."

I realise that you may be uncomfortable saying "That's right" or "Yes" to something that is wrong (in your world).

If this is the case, begin by simply acknowledging the validity of the other person's input. You do not have to agree – you simply need to acknowledge that, in their world, they are right and their contribution is valuable. By taking a moment to communicate that you have evaluated what they have said positively before adding your perspective you will maintain an agreeable and influential dynamic.

"I can see how you have come to that conclusion, so what if we look at it like this..."

"OK, I'm with you, and now let's get to grips with how we can make that realistic..."

Simply by acknowledging the other person's point they will 'feel' that you have listened to them and considered what they are saying.

It is important that your voice tone and body language is reflecting this agreement. Nodding your head makes this pattern easier to deliver, and a nod alone can be the agreement. By simply pausing and nodding, you have demonstrated respect for the other person's model of the world, and you can go on to contradict it with little resistance.

How the listener 'feels' about the communication will strongly influence what they will take from it – what they will accept or reject.

By maintaining the 'feeling' of agreement, the conversation will remain productive – adding to rather than contradicting and arguing.

When you maintain agreement, you are maintaining your influence.

Your turn

In the following exercise, imagine that the comments below have been said to you by another person.

I would like you to prepare a response for each that will guide the speaker to be more resourceful or flexible using one, two or all of the following:

- Pre-frame (and bringing people back to the intention or desired outcome)
- Softening
- Maintaining Agreement

"All salesmen would sell their grandmother."

"No, I don't care, he's wrong, that's all there is to it."

"It's not my fault, it's hers, I don't see how it's my problem, why should I stay and work late?"

"The deadline is unrealistic."

Before even thinking about beginning to introduce The Milton Model, there is one more Big Idea that I need to share with you.

Meaning of the communication is the response you get

It doesn't matter what you say, as long as you get the right response. If you get the wrong response, it doesn't matter what you meant.

The map is not the territory, and words are completely unreliable, so, respecting that we all live in different worlds, the technical correctness of the words you choose (as you understand them) is irrelevant.

When you communicate, the meaning that has been communicated is the meaning that is received by the other person. Like it or not, that is what has happened.

If the meaning they receive is different to the meaning you intended,

161

then the meaning you intended is not what you communicated. In order to become an exceptional communicator, you need to calibrate on the results you are getting.

It doesn't matter how clearly you understand your point, or how clearly you thought you communicated it, if the listener did not understand then you have not communicated it clearly in their world.

For example: In the early 90's when computers were relatively new in the workplace, I handed a floppy disc to my PA and said, "Please copy this for me, hang on to the copy and send the original out in the mail."

I remember the disc clearly; it was black with a white label that I had written on in blue pen. A week or so later I asked for the copy of the disk and she handed me a sheet of A4 paper with a photocopied image of the disc on it.

I was speechless and a little annoyed. I look back on that interaction now and ask myself what would have happened if I had said, "Please put this disc in your computer and replicate it before sending the original out in the mail."

I would have got a different response.

I was the one communicating the request, I was the one that created ambiguity and left out details, I was the one that did not confirm that she had understood my request, so really it was my responsibility, and therefore my error.

This also works the other way. If it gets the right result, you need to have the flexibility to communicate in whatever way is necessary, regardless of whether that communication is technically right or wrong.

Earlier in the book I asked you to realise that the dictionary is unreliable, now I'm asking you to become less rigid about correct grammar. When it comes to speaking (which is a very different medium to writing) I would like you to forget all of the 'rules' that you were taught in language lessons.

The patterns of the Milton Model rely upon you making grammatical errors and developing a level of flexibility in your communication that generates the responses and results that you want.

The Milton Model

This next section will define and provide examples of all the patterns of the Milton Model.

In my opinion, this model is an auditory experience, and as such needs to be experienced in that modality.

If you are reading this as an introduction to NLP, I'm sure that you will find value in some of the techniques. To gain an experience of these patterns working, I suggest that, after completing this section, you listen to a hypnotic CD with the intention of spotting and identifying the patterns used.

If you are reading this as pre-study material for a course, then it will bring the patterns into your awareness, making them easy to hear when you do experience them, and provide reference material for during and after the course.

As you read through the following patterns, imagine hearing them. Create the sounds in your mind. This will allow you to see how they work by getting a feel for what they would sound like.

You're not going to make me behave like a chicken are you?

There is an enormous amount of misconception about what hypnosis really is.

This is mainly due to the format in which most people are aware of it – hypnotic stage shows. There is a perception of loss of control; that the hypnotist has some kind of power over you, can tell you to do anything and you are powerless to resist.

I can promise you that, during a hypnotic stage show, the people on stage entertaining their friends by being a chicken want to entertain their friends by being a chicken.

The hypnotist takes care to select willing subjects and in many cases it is questionable whether the individual is even in a trance.

Hypnosis is not something that you do **to** people, it's something that you do **with** people.

OK, it can be used as a 'trick' to get a certain short term result, but it is not possible to enforce your will upon another person, and a hypnotised subject will not accept a suggestion that is not OK with them.

It works by making suggestions that require the client to 'go inside' to find the answer.

If you were to practise hypnotherapy, you would be amazed to find how inexpensive the professional liability insurance is. You can be covered for £1,000,000.00 for just £60 per year. Why do you think that is? Surely if you are 'messing with people's brains' it would be far more expensive.

The truth is; you cannot do anything to your client. You can only make suggestions that the client can accept or reject, and they will only accept the suggestions that are right for them.

The more permissive and vague the suggestion is, the more agreeable it is. The moment you provide a suggestion that the client rejects, the spell is broken.

So for hypnosis to work, the hypnotist creates an extremely comfortable atmosphere of rapport and makes suggestions that are agreeable, easy to accept and right for the client. It is a highly ecological process. If a therapist were to attempt to simply tell his client what to do, the command would be rejected.[*]

For example, if I were to say to you, "I wonder how your foot feels against your shoe," you have to 'go inside' to find an experience to attach to that sentence.

I have just guided your experience. I have drawn your attention to the feeling of your foot against your shoe. (Presupposing that you are wearing shoes.)

I did not tell you to do it; I simply made a softened suggestion. The soft and permissive nature of the comment makes it almost irresistible.

If I were to say, "Get a sensation of your foot against your shoe." That sentence may still work, however it's less agreeable and therefore easier to resist. You are likely to think "No", or "Why?"

Furthermore, there is still much debate over what hypnotic trance really is. My understanding is that it's induction or utilization of a naturally occurring state. We go into trances all the time.

Have you ever found yourself drifting in your thoughts and staring at a fixed place without really looking at it? Have you been driving and not remembered parts of your journey? These are everyday examples of this naturally occurring state called trance.

So how is this useful in your everyday life?

How much more engaging and motivational will your speech be when you can use language patterns that are extremely agreeable,

---

[*] There are some authoritarian styles of hypnosis that are more commanding, however there are still limits to what you can tell a subject to do.

bypassing the listeners' filtering processes, and provide suggestions that guide the listeners' experience?

As you work through these patterns, you will begin to realise that you need to be very respectful of the listener's model of the world and flexible in you communication to achieve this level of influence.

So how does it work?

Having created an unconscious feeling of rapport between you and the listener, and maintaining that rapport (we will cover how to achieve this later) there are three things that cause your communication to be hypnotic.

1. Pacing the listener's current experience and speaking in such a way that the listener has no option but to think 'yes' to everything you are saying

2. Overloading the listeners' conscious mind so that they stop consciously and deductively filtering and evaluating what you are saying

3. Using ambiguous words that require the listener to 'go inside' to find a meaning and providing suggestions and presuppositions that are easy for the listener to accept

As we work through each pattern of the Milton Model, I would like you to make a note of what you think the effect of the pattern is.

The upside-down Meta Model

Firstly, the Milton Model contains all of the patterns of the Meta Model 'in reverse'.

The Meta Model identifies speech patterns that have distorted, deleted and generalised information.

The Milton Model uses distortions, deletions and generalisations to create ambiguity and deliver presuppositions.

Whereas, in the Meta Model, these patterns are violations that lead to misunderstanding, in the Milton Model they are used to manage the listener's experience – knowing that the listener will allocate their own meaning to patterns, and utilising that process.

Allow me to elaborate before we move on to the specific patterns.

165

For example – let's imagine that I want to make the following explicit point:

"It is important that your brand and corporate identity is consistent."

I may say something like:

"Think of a brand that is synonymous with quality, a brand that you associate with credibility and professionalism. Now just allow yourself to think of some of the many times you have seen that brand and notice how consistent it looks and how consistently it is treated every time you come into contact with it."

So I've just made my point.

What's interesting is that; I have no idea what brand you used to support my point. I used the nominalized words 'quality', 'credibility' and 'professionalism' and you allocated your meaning to those words and then selected a brand.

I have no idea what the brand is – but I do know that it is the most appropriate brand to support what I was saying – because you chose it.

You have chosen the best example to convince yourself of my point. This is far more influential than any example that I could choose.

I am utilising your experience; your 'model of the world'.

If I had added in my own specific example of a brand you may not have agreed with me. It may have been a brand that you do not associate with quality.

By being more vague and permissive I have made my point more convincing to you. People often believe that, in order to be convincing you need to provide a lot of accurate information.

More specific information provides more opportunity for disagreement. When communicating influentially – LESS IS MORE. This is literally true – the less information you provide, the more the listener needs to add to make sense of it – and the meaning they add will make what you are saying make sense to them.

The first patterns of the Milton Model that I will share with you are the Meta Model patterns that we have already covered, demonstrating how they can be used to manage the listener's experience:

Nominalizations

I have provided an example of using nominalisations above. The listener will attribute their meaning to the nominalization, and they need to 'go inside' to find this meaning – thus you are influencing their attention direction and their therefore their experience.

Think of the most important **learnings** you have already gained from this book.

You have to go inside and allocate your personal experience to the word learnings in order for the word to have meaning.

Some of your **communication** can improve with this pattern.

Your turn. Use a Nominalization to guide the listener's experience:

_____

_____

_____

Mind Reading

"I know you are wondering..."

If you can guess what's going on in the other person's mind – and get it right – it's extremely engaging.

So how do you guess what's going on in someone else's mind and get it right?

Easy – don't be specific about it, just stick to the obvious things and don't specify. Pace what you can see their current experience is.

For example: "I know you are wondering...." And leave it at that. Do not be specific about what they are wondering – you are simply indicating that you know that's what they are doing.

Now, I know what you are thinking, and you may be right.

Again; the sentence above suggests that I know what you are thinking – of course I have no idea.

"I know why you are here..."

"I can see that you are excited..."

"I can hear what you want to say...."

"I know what you mean..." (and of course you don't)

Your turn. I know you can create your own Mind Read:

_____

_____

_____

Cause-Effect

"If you are reading this book, then you are learning the effect of certain words."

The first part of the sentence is true and paces their current experience, so the second part of the sentence becomes easy to accept. To demonstrate this:

"If you are reading this book then you can notice how the paper feels"

You can use the second part of the sentence however you wish as long as it is agreeable to the listener:

"**If** you are reading this book **then**......(*Whatever you want the listener to think*)"

"Reading this book **makes** you....,.....(*Whatever you want the listener to think*)"

"**If** you attend an NLP Practitioner Course, you will become competent in all of these patterns". (*This sentence will work if you are attending an NLP Practitioner course*).

Your Turn. If you create an example then you will become more aware of the pattern.

_____

_____

_____

Complex Equivalence

"Reading this book means that you are learning."

I am providing you with a meaning for reading this book. You will 'go inside' to attach your experience to that meaning, and, if it is acceptable, you will accept it.

We will allocate a meaning to anything that comes to our conscious attention. We generally do this very quickly however if it is something unusual, unexpected, puzzling or ambiguous we may have to think a bit in order to do this. If someone kindly provides us with a meaning for confusing or ambiguous information, we find it very easy to accept.

"You are reading about NLP which **means** that you are open-minded."

"Learning the Milton Model **means** that you can become an influential speaker."

Your Turn. That means you can create an example.

Presuppositions (not covered elsewhere in this model)

In the Meta Model we indicated that many sentences contain an assumption made by the speaker.

You are very sensitive to and aware of these assumptions even if you cannot explicitly define them yet. You would not be able to communicate with others at such a 'surface' level unless you were responding to the presuppositions within their patterns of speech.

In order to make sense of the speaker's words we are required to accept the things that they are presupposing. Without noticing and accepting presuppositions, the sentence does not work or will be rejected.

I was sitting on the train this morning thinking of how to begin to explain a presupposition when a voice over the loud speaker said, "Mind the gap."

As I sat there in the train, I had accepted the existence of a gap between the train and the platform. I was expecting there to be one. If there were no gap I would be surprised.

The voice did not say, "There is a gap between the train and the platform." It did not need to. The sentence, "Mind the gap," presupposes the existence of the gap.

The sentence only 'works' if there is a gap between the train and the platform. If you were to step off the train and there were no gap you may be surprised as you were expecting there to be one. This particular example is a presupposition of existence. The speaker is presupposing that the gap exists and bringing that existence into your awareness.

169

Presupposition of existence

By presupposing the existence of something (often a noun), the speaker is likely to accept that it exists and will imagine it, or if it is present, you can draw their attention to it.

"Mind the gap." *(Presupposing there is a gap.)*

"I cycle to work." *(Presupposing there is a bicycle and a place of work.)*

"Put the book on the table." *(Presupposing there is a book and a table.)*

Your turn. Draw the listener's attention to the existence of something:

_____

_____

_____

Presupposition of awareness

This makes the listener AWARE of something:

"Can you **hear** the sounds around you?"

"You can **notice** how you are **feeling**..."

The presupposition that the listener can become aware of sounds and feelings (or any of the 5 senses) will draw their attention to them.

Your turn. Draw the listener's attention to a sensory stimulus:

_____

_____

_____

Adjective/adverb

The presupposition indicated by an adjective/adverb can be used to manage the listener's perception:

"You are reading these **powerful** patterns."

Because the statement that you are reading these patterns is a fact, the word powerful becomes linked to that fact and, as long as the adjective is not unacceptable to the listener, will be easily accepted.

"Sit in this **comfortable** chair."

Provided that there is a chair, you will expect it to be comfortable.

Your turn. Create a factual sentence that includes an adverb/adjective. You can create an **excellent** example as **quickly** as you wish.

_____

_____

_____

Presupposition of time

These are particularly useful, and we use them more often that you would imagine.

"When will you **stop** worrying about small details?" *(Presupposing that you are doing it at the moment.)*

"You **had** a problem with presentations." *(Presupposing that you no longer have the problem. It's in the past.)*

Your turn. Have you thought of an example yet?

_____

_____

_____

A presupposition using **OR** is a **'double bind'**.

"I don't know if you will complete this section now or at another time." *(Either way I'm presupposing that you will complete it).*

This is the classic salesman's close:

"Do you want it in blue or red?" *(Presupposing that the client wants it – moves their attention to selecting the colour.)*

"Will you sign the order with my pen or yours?" *(Presupposing that you will sign the order.)*

Notice how the listener's attention moves to making the decision 'blue or red'; 'now or at another time' and away from what is being presupposed. If you are thinking about whether you want it in 'blue or red', you must have accepted that you want it.

You do not need to include all of the options. I could ask:

"Do you want it in blue or another colour?" *(I'm still presupposing that the client wants it, and moving their attention to selecting the colour without needing to limit myself to blue or red.)*

"Are you going to do that now or later?" *(Either way you are doing it.)*

Your turn. Will you create your own example immediately or after some thought?

An **ordinal presupposition** can be used to suggest what will happen next.

"Come in, sit down and make yourself comfortable."

Because they are coming into the room, and they are about to sit down, they will be open to whatever the next suggestion is. The first two suggestions are correct and agreeable so 'it follows that' the next one will be.

You can use a list, or numbers to make an ordinal presupposition.

I often refer to my wife Helen as 'my first wife Helen'. This joke works because calling Helen my first wife presupposes that I will have another.

When I finish this book I will start my third one. *(Presupposing that this is the second and there was a book before this one.)*

Your turn. Read this sentence, reflect for a moment and then create your own example:

Universal Quantifiers

This pattern is fairly obvious. Notice how the examples below are just easy to read. They are generally agreeable.

"**We all** like to be understood when we communicate."

"**Everyone** can think of a time when they were misunderstood."

"Learning a new skill is **always** empowering."

Your turn. Anyone can make their own examples below:

_____

_____

_____

Modal Operators of Possibility

If there are two words that you can begin using right now, they are 'you can'.

I find these words extremely influential, mainly because they are so agreeable.

For example:

If I were to say, "You will continue reading this book," you may think 'no I won't, how do you know? Don't tell me what I will do.'

If I were to say, "You can continue reading this book," this is a fact – you can, can't you? It is almost impossible to disagree – I am simply making you aware of the possibility. It would be extremely difficult to disagree.

However, in making you aware of the possibility, I am making a suggestion, for you to continue reading the book. The words 'you can' are both agreeable and empowering to the listener, and as such the suggestion can be extremely influential.

"**You can** notice how simple this model is when you take one pattern at a time."

"**It is possible to** hear the sounds around you now."

***Your turn.* You can** allow your mind to wonder, creating your own examples:

_____

_____

_____

Lost Performative

As you provide a listener with confusing or ambiguous information, they are wondering what to make of it, so if you tell them what to make of it your value judgements will meet little resistance.

"Thus using this pattern with people **is a good thing**."

"**It's bad** to be manipulative."

"**It's important** that you create your own examples."

Your turn. It's good to create an example:

_____

_____

_____

Deletions – using ambiguity

When you delete information and you are in rapport with the listener, they will look for reason and meaning to support the unqualified or unspecified statement.

Notice how, if the listener does not challenge the deletion, they can easily accept the deleted statements without knowing what they mean – they will attribute their own meaning that supports the deleted statement.

For example: If I were to say, "The patterns that make sense immediately", I have not specified which pattern they are, so you will allocate the meaning that is correct for you – the patterns that you found to make sense immediately.

In using deletions, you can be artfully vague, providing the listener with the latitude to allocate their own specific meanings and find their own specific examples within the parameters of what you are communicating.

Because you are using their examples, and their meanings, they will always be correct to the listener.

Simple Deletions

"I'm **confident**."
"I'm **empowered**."
"I **feel sure**."

Your turn. And you?

_____

_____

_____

Comparative deletions

"Learning NLP this way is **better**."
"This pattern is even **more effective**."
"Your communication will be **more resourceful**."

Your turn. Your next example will be an improvement:

_____

_____

_____

Lack of referential Index

(Unspecified nouns and verbs)

"**People** can learn a lot from NLP."
"**Many patterns** are extremely empowering in business."
"**They** will notice **a difference**."

Your turn. It will be easy now:

_____

_____

_____

It's Playtime

So, having noticed how the distortions, generalisations and deletions can be used to influence the listener, you can begin to become aware of some of the further patterns of the Milton Model.

As mentioned earlier, to successfully utilise the Milton Model you will need to accept that the spoken word is very different to the written word.

Many of these patterns will not work in writing, because they simply look wrong.

Speech is not scrutinised in the same way as written text. You can 'get away with' errors in speech that can be extremely effective in managing the listener's experience.

I would invite you to approach the Milton Model as playfully as possible. You can treat it as a game or whatever you need to do to develop the behavioural flexibility and be comfortable causing the kind of effects listed at the beginning of this section.

Tag Questions

Tag questions are an extremely easy-to-use technique. I'm sure you can think of how people use them in everyday speech, can't you?

They are a question, and should therefore be quite soft and permissive, because that will usually get an agreeable response, won't it?

And people use these every day, don't they?

When they are written they don't really work, do they? They're a bit too obvious, aren't they? And they can be so easy to use in speech, can't they?

Your turn. you can create one, can't you? It's easy, isn't it?

_____

_____

_____

Pacing Current Experience

How easy is it to state the obvious? Again this is an extremely easy and powerful pattern.

Simply tell the listener what they are experiencing. It really is as easy as that:

For example: "As you read this page...."

Obviously I would need to be able to observe your experience to feed it back to you. I know you are reading this page. However, I'm unable to observe anything else as I write this page several weeks or months ago.

I would need to be with you to utilise this pattern.

For example, if I can see that you are sitting down, I could say, "You are sitting down," or, "As you sit in the chair...."

I'm sure you can guess what this pattern achieves.

Your turn. Make a note of an experience that you can observe in your listener, and then construct a sentence that feeds that experience back to them – stating the obvious. Create a couple of examples:

_____

_____

_____

Embedded Commands

Are you aware of how the intonation of a sentence has an effect on the way we process it as a listener?

Personally, I find it strange the way that many of the people I have met from Australia have an upward intonation at the end of their sentences. It has the effect of turning the sentence into a question even if it's a statement. Some young people in the UK seem to do the same thing.

Take the statement, "I went to the garage."

Now imagine hearing it with an upward tonality, so the speaker's voice goes up in tone at the end of the sentence.

It somehow makes the speaker sound unsure, or sounds as if they are asking a question of the listener. It's a question tonality. I find myself thinking 'are you telling me this or asking me?'

As you have already noticed, voice tone is extremely important in terms of how the words are processed by the listener. There are three different intonations that we will look at here:

1. Question tonality
2. Statement tonality
3. Command tonality

Now, how good is your imagination for creating sounds in your mind?

Below are a few examples that we already looked at in 'softening frames' earlier in this chapter. In each case, imagine how the sentence would sound if the underlined content (1) went up in tone (2) stayed at the same level or (3) went down in tone.

"I'm just wondering if you can <u>do that for me now</u>."

"It's interesting if you <u>pay attention to this now</u>, you can…"

"I don't know when you will <u>notice that this is very important</u>."

Were you able to imagine the different delivery of the sentence, and therefore the different meaning in the listener's mind?

This pattern is best when delivered extremely subtly. The listener will consciously think you have asked them a permissive question; unconsciously they will respond to the question according to the tonality used.

If you are able to employ a command tonality, your permissive questions will meet little resistance and be responded to as if they were a command.

Conversational Postulate

A conversational postulate is simply a 'modal operator' question that works as a command.

For example, if I were to say, "Can you shut the door?" You would be unlikely to reply, you would simply shut the door. You would take a question and react to it as if it were a request, as if I had said, "Please shut the door."

However, as it is a question, it is softer and more agreeable.

Examples of questions that begin with or contain modal operators are: 'can you...?', 'will you...?', 'would you...?', 'should you...?'.

For example: "Can you imagine how this will work?"

Create your own examples below:

_____

_____

_____

You can make this even more effective by adding an 'improper pause'. We will cover improper pauses separately – for now, notice what happens when you pause half way through this sentence:

"Can you imagine?............how this will work?"

"Can you hear?............the sounds around you?"

The listener thinks 'yes' to the first part of the sentence, and is therefore in a 'yes' mindset to receive the second part of the sentence.

Can you think?...................of an example?

"Quotes"

An interesting thing happens when you tell someone what someone else said.

You realise consciously that you are being told a quote; however you will unconsciously react to the sentence as if it were said to you directly.

For example: "I was in a meeting and, out of the blue, someone said, 'Notice how the paper feels against your thumb,' and I thought that was an odd thing to say."

Notice what happens – you are likely to process the information as if it is directed at you. When you read the example above, did you become aware of how your thumb felt against the paper?

This is a very practical pattern in business. It reduces the resistance in the listener because they think you are speaking about someone else when you are, in reality, speaking directly to them. This is the power of testimonials.

Another example would be, "My brother read this book and said it was the most practical presentation of NLP he had ever seen."

Your turn. The first time that I was shown this technique the trainer said, "You can create your own example now."

_____

_____

_____

Extended quotes can be used to further reduce the 'filtering' of the conscious mind by adding a couple of layers of detail to the quotation: For example:

"I was meeting a client last week and while waiting in reception the receptionist told me that she had heard the Managing Director talking to HR Director who said that **my training is highly effective**."

The conscious mind becomes occupied with the structure of the quote and the message of the quote is processed without resistance.

Selectional Restriction Violation

In this pattern you talk about objects or animals as if they have human behaviours or feelings.

Like the bottle of red wine that sometimes calls out to me from the wine rack after a long week at work.

Get the idea? Some more examples would be:

"I wonder how the room feels."

"The report told me something I had not noticed."

"The chair is feeling comfortable."

Your turn. Your pen can write down an example:

_____

Ambiguity

We have already looked at how powerful ambiguous speech is when you are being artfully vague and the listener attributes their own meaning.

As well as sentences where the meaning is unspecified or unqualified, some sentences can be ambiguous by having multiple possible meanings.

Four such patterns are listed below:

Phonological Ambiguity

As you are aware, many different words 'sound' the same.

Two / To / Too

There / Their

I'm sure you can think of a few more.

You can utilise this ambiguity to make your speech deliberately confusing.

For example:

"My son is shining today."

"This is important for getting everything you don't need to remember."

"Your unconscious knows it can 'sniff out' the answer."

Your turn. You can create your own example:

_____

Syntactic Ambiguity

Syntactic ambiguity is created when it is impossible to determine the function of a word in a sentence.

For example: "They are managing managers."

Are they managing people who are managers, or are they managers that are managing?

"In NLP we are communicating people."

Are we communicating the topic of people or are we people who are communicating?

"They are visiting colleagues who work in other offices."

Are they away visiting colleagues or are they colleagues who are visiting?

Your turn. Make a learning example for interesting listeners:

_____

Ambiguity of Scope

Scope ambiguity makes it unclear how much part of the sentence applies to the other part of the sentence.

For example: "All the beautiful women and men"
Are the men and women beautiful, or is it just the women?
"The HR Managers and secretaries"
Do the secretaries work in HR or is it all secretaries?
"Speaking to you as someone on an NLP journey"
Is that you or me?

Your turn. Think of interesting examples and phrases:

Ambiguity of Punctuation

There are two ambiguity patterns that are described as 'punctuation'.
Firstly, **run on sentences**:
"As you read this work book yourself on an NLP course."
"Can I ask you something personal change is very empowering."
"As you sit on this chair a meeting using these skills in the future."

Your turn. Create some examples are useful.

The second pattern is **improper pauses:**
"Can I borrow your watch...........ful attention?"
"And now you're unconscious............. mind can find the answer"
"They will not fail............. to make a mess of it"
"Make time to stop and think......................... of an example."

Putting it together

I know you're wondering,

    ...and it's a good thing to wonder,

    ...how you can begin to experience the Milton Model in practice

    ...the patterns, then they will become natural, and feel good,

    ...and that means you can use them

    ...all the time.

I don't know if you will use them immediately, or later

    ...and either way, you can begin to notice them.

We all use this language every day

    ...and as you read this page... can show you

so you can begin to, hear, make yourself aware of the many things you have learned...

It's great for 'confusing people'...

...and you can use it when talking to two people too, or even more than that...

...so that means you can imagine how it will help you when you are speaking in many ways.

It's interesting, isn't it, how easily you can, can you not, just be artfully vague...

...and that means you can relax and enjoy the things you are leaving out...

...and the many other things that you have already noticed you can do...

...because I know that you now know that it's about the enjoyable effects of many things.

Make a note of the patterns you have noticed used above and mark where you could use a command tonality.

Summary

In this section you have constructed:

- Pre-Frames
- Softening Frames
- Frames for maintaining agreement
- Milton Model Patterns.

I would urge you to practise by writing a paragraph of speech to a colleague. Be clear about your intention in the communication, soften the message and then add in as many Milton Model patterns as you possibly can, can you not?

If you wish to develop a level of ability that will allow you to reliably utilise these patterns a great deal of practice in usually required. The more time you can spend with someone that has already mastered this skill the more easily you can assimilate this model.

I practised constructing Milton Model patterns obsessively for years, at any opportunity, driving in my car, on the toilet, before I went to sleep at night, and I use at least one pattern in almost every conversation that I have.

Notice that the consistent intended dynamic throughout this chapter is agreement on the part of the listener. When the dynamic of agreement is present, and the listener thinks 'yes' you are being influential. It is difficult to be influential under the conditions of disagreement.

6. Negotiation

My friend John was working with some people who realised that he was particularly gifted at map reading.

He could negotiate rough terrain in the darkest of night with almost zero visibility. Other map readers were unable to get the same results – perhaps they were having trouble distinguishing between the map and the territory?

John told me that he would find characteristics on the map that he could be aware of in reality (the sounds from a trickle of a stream or the crackle of a power line) that marked useful boundaries; and he knew that, as long has he negotiated the territory within those parameters he would find his objective, with all the flexibility of lateral movement in between.

I suppose the first question I would ask you is, "What is negotiation?"

I'm not sure how you would define it. I would say it's the process of interaction between different parties to reach an agreement.

Two people enter a negotiation with differing objectives or agendas, and the process of negotiation arrives at an outcome that is then agreed by all parties.

When you think about it, many of the interactions we have on a day-to-day basis can be described this way.

I know that, now that we have a baby, I negotiate with my wife for a night out with my friends.

Take a moment to think of the many conversations you have that are actually negotiations. Both parties may have different objectives and the outcome needs to be decided and agreed upon.

There is a perception that negotiation is in some way competitive or confrontational. Almost as if for you to win the other person must lose. Is this really necessary?

Have you ever found yourself in a position where the only realistic option is to say, "OK, we seem to have reached a stalemate – can we start again?"

This win/lose approach is caused by people entering into a negotiation with a rigid and fixed outcome. They have decided in advance the outcome that they want, and they will attempt to get it without compromise. If they get it they win, if they don't they lose.

Why bother? This is not a negotiation; it's a battle of wills or an argument.

It's certainly not worth meeting – you may as well do this via email. Simply state your outcome and 'stick to your guns' – why discuss it if it's not flexible?

If you were to negotiate your way across some rough terrain, you would expect to move left and right as well as forwards. Fixing your vision on a point on the horizon and marching forward may not be the best approach.

If the people with whom you are negotiating are people who you are required to or hope to have an ongoing relationship with, it does you no favours to 'get one over on them'.

To do so would simply cultivate a relationship of resentment. They will certainly not 'go the extra mile' for you if they feel that you have taken advantage of them – you have won and they have lost.

In applying this negotiation model, I have presupposed that the objective of the negotiation is to find a mutually agreeable and beneficial outcome.

It is important that I make this distinction – because it is not always the case.

Through coaching, and exploring negotiation styles with my clients, there are some circumstances where the individual has the objective of gaining as much ground as possible over the other party, regardless of any consequences.

For example, one of my clients negotiates the sale of businesses. His brief is to get as much money as possible for the business. The people with whom he is negotiating are hoping to drive the price down as far as possible. He has no other considerations. There is no future relationship to consider. When the business is sold the current shareholders want as much money as possible, future relationships are unimportant. The deal is done the moment the paper is signed and he moves on to the next one. His objective is dictated from someone else. It's just about the numbers.

Well, I suppose I am happy to concede that in cases such as this, where both parties perceive the negotiation as a fight, the win/lose approach seems correct – or maybe I should call it the 'win regardless' approach.

I would, however, suggest that, in such scenarios the negotiation is defensive or aggressive and either one or both parties will often need to concede something for an agreement to be found. So what was the point of the rigid stance? It did not work.

Being rigid does not make the other party say "OK then".

Even in these scenarios, when the objective is to get the best outcome with no further or future considerations, is it possible that working cooperatively within certain parameters would be a more efficient and reliable approach? Just an idea.

Assuming that you see the merit of maintaining agreement while negotiating within certain framed parameters; then I will move on. Remember, in negotiation, as with any other application of NLP, without rapport and agreement there can be no influence.

Also, I would again ask you the question: "Is a person persuaded or motivated for your reasons, or their own?"

If they are motivated by their own reasons, how can you influence them if you are engaged in a battle? If there is a dynamic of disagreement they will be resistant to your ideas.

By definition, an effective negotiation requires some degree of movement.

The negotiation model in this section is underpinned by a couple of important 'Big Ideas':

The person with the most flexibility exercises the most influence

This is the **Law of Requisite Variety**.

If you are flexible about an outcome, it provides you with the flexibility to exercise choice over your communication, and thus you are able to exercise more influence.

Have you ever been in a negotiation when one person has been rigid and inflexible? They are 'stuck' in their only acceptable outcome; they do not exercise choice over how they communicate and are not influential.

Besides, if you go into a negotiation without flexibility, how do you know you are right? Surely, on some occasions, someone else will have a better suggestion. How will you know if you do not have the flexibility to let go of your own suggestion for a moment. Can you accept that your position cannot always be right?

Let's imagine that I take you to a Cup Final football match. I'm going to provide a couple of scenarios for the purpose of comparison:

In the first scenario, you are a fanatical supporter of one of the teams. You have two possible outcomes:

1. Your team wins.
2. Your team loses.

Notice that this has nothing to do with which is the best team on the day. In this scenario you are not concerned with what is fair or right.

In the second scenario, you are not a supporter of either team. You are there 'for the love of the game', simply hoping to enjoy watching a good match and 'may the best team win'.

How much more likely are you to have an outcome that is acceptable to you when you have this amount of flexibility over the outcome?

So how does this make a difference in the context of influence or negotiation? As we considered earlier, in order to have influence there needs to be agreement – as soon as the feeling of agreement is broken, the other party will begin to evaluate and filter the information they receive more critically. They may stop listening as they construct their counter argument.

The more rigid or fixed you are in your ideas, opinions or suggestions, the more opportunity there is for disagreement. The more disagreement, the less cooperative and influential the communication becomes.

All behaviour
functions from
positive intention

It is also very resourceful to be aware that, generally speaking nobody gets out of bed in the morning and thinks 'who's day can I mess up?' or 'how can I ruin my career today?'

When entering a negotiation it serves you well to realise that the other person is operating from positive intentions for themselves, rather than negative intentions for you.

It may be important to them to 'win' – that does not mean it's important that you lose. In NLP we choose to presuppose that **all** behaviour functions from a positive intention for the individual.

OK, sometimes we get it wrong. We adopt behaviours that do not help us, or are in some way destructive, but the intention behind the behaviour is usually positive.

This is extremely important when facilitating behavioural change in yourself or others. More on that later...

One 'chunk' at a time

In this chapter we will look at managing negotiation by controlling the level of detail at which the other person is communicating (and therefore thinking).

You can use linguistic framing to pre-frame the negotiation and maintain agreement throughout. You can also move the negotiation to a more abstract or more specific place using Milton Model Patterns, Meta Model Questions and some 'chunking' questions that I will provide.

'Chunking' is the process of moving the listener's attention and thinking from one logical level to another.

The best way to illustrate logical levels is to provide an example. In the model below is a representation of the topic of cars, the more abstract logical levels above it and the more detailed logical levels below it.

Happy / Fulfilled Life

↑↓

Travel / Get around

↑↓

Transport

↑↓

Cars

↓↑

BMW

↓↑

3 series

↓↑

330i

In the diagram above the topic (cars) is in bold. The topics above the word cars are more abstract – at a higher logical level – those below are more detailed – at a lower logical level.

If you say 'BMW' you are being more explicit or detailed than if you say 'car' – which could be any make of car. This is a logical levels hierarchy.

It's a hierarchy because, at each lower logical level there are more options, more members of the set. For example:

Cars

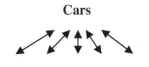

Audi Ford BMW VW   Lexus

Within the 'set' of cars, there are many specific types of cars. They are all cars; they are simply more specific descriptions. Thus, they are members of the 'set' called 'cars'.

Similarly, 'cars' are a member of the 'set' called 'transport':

Transport

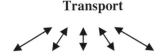

Buses Boats **Cars** Trains Aeroplanes

At each logical level of detail, there are more options at a lower logical level, and fewer options at a higher logical level.

It's also important that, as we move down through the logical levels, becoming more specific, we are still talking about the same thing – each lower level inherits all of the characteristics that define the 'set' and adds more detail.

For example:

Cars
↓
BMW
↓
3 series
↓
330i

So starting from **Cars**:

Think of the characteristics or boundary conditions that define a car. (4 wheels, steering wheel, engine etc.) By the way, notice that these defining conditions are not absolute – the word car is a metaphor for things that fit the intuitive idea of what constitutes a car and the boundary conditions are unspecific.

As we become more specific, moving down a level to BMW are we still talking about cars? Is a BMW a car? Yes! Have we inherited all of the characteristics of the 'set' description cars? (4 wheels etc)Yes.

And so on. At the next level – Is a 3 series still a BMW? Yes.

Is a 3 series still a car? Yes.

How about the level of description that identifies the specific model of car?

Is a 330i still a 3 series?

Is a 330i still a BMW?

Is a 330i still a car?

Yes, yes and yes.

Also note the constriction of possible alternatives as we move down in levels of detail. For example:

1. How many cars are there in your country?
2. How many BMWs are there in your country?

Notice that the answer to question 2 must be a lower number than question 1, because question 2 relates to a sub-set of question 1. There are many sub-sets, so the number of options at the more specific level of detail must be substantially less than at the higher logical level.

How many 3 series are there?

Again, not all BMWs are 3 series, so there must be a greater number of BMWs in general than there are 3 series BMWs.

So we have noticed two things that happen as you move down in logical levels, becoming more specific:

- Firstly – each time you become more specific, the new subject inherits all of the defining characteristics of the level above. (A BMW is still a car).
- Secondly – each time you become more specific you are constraining your options. Quite obvious when you think about it; more specific = less options or possibilities.

Obviously, the reverse is also true:

As you move up in logical levels (from BMW to Cars) you are creating a broader description and therefore generating more options and possibilities.

(i.e. If you have confined you choice to BMWs you have less options than if you have only confined your choice to 'cars').

Also, as you move up a logical level you let go of details that exist at a lower level. If you were to list the criterion that makes something a BMW, in moving up a level, you are preserving only the criterion that makes it a Car, and therefore discarding some of the more specific BMW details.

This is an important point in terms of negotiation, the process of 'letting go' of some specific criterion.

A note on personality...

Something that I often encounter in coaching scenarios; a common 'problem' is a miss match in the levels of detail that people think and communicate at.

One person may be addressing an issue from a very detailed perspective, the other from a far more 'big picture' point of view. Some people tend to see 'the wood', others notice the details of 'the trees'.

This is one of Carl Jung's 'Personality Types': Some people are 'Sensors' – detail focused with less attention to 'bigger issues', and others are 'Intuitors' – 'big picture' thinkers with less attention to detail. This is true in my experience in observing people 'chunking' and finding it challenging to move in one direction or the other. A few people have the ability to comfortably move from one extreme to another.

Awareness of, and linguistic control of, logical levels is extremely effective in communicating with people who are thinking at a different logical level to you.

For example, if someone is very detail focused, you can 'chunk them up' to a more intuitive level of thinking.

Similarly, if someone is thinking on a 'big picture' level and paying no attention to detail you can 'chunk them down' to more specific information.

If someone were to stop and ask you for directions to a place, you would not simply provide a detailed description of what the destination looks like. You would need to start from where they are now and direct them to the next street; and the next street and so on.

Simply telling them to look at things at a different logical level will have no effect. In order to 'chunk' someone up or down you must start from where they are currently and move them from there one chunk at a time.

So how can you easily move people up and down in logical levels?

Chunking Questions

To chunk up, simply ask:

- What's the intention?
- What's the purpose?

So let's use these questions and see what happens:

What's the intention of cars? – Transport

What's the purpose of cars? – Transport

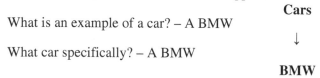

Transport

↑

Cars

To chunk down, ask:

- What are examples of this?
- Any Meta Model Question: (How, What, Who, When) Specifically?

So let's use these questions and see what happens:

What is an example of a car? – A BMW

What car specifically? – A BMW

Cars

↓

BMW

To chunk sideways, chunk up and then ask for another example.

- What's the Purpose of cars? – Transport
- What's another example of a type of Transport? – Trains

Transport

↑   ↓

Cars   Trains

In terms of interaction – chunking up will make the topic more agreeable.

Chunking down makes the topic more specific and therefore there are more details to disagree with.

For example, if we need to agree on a type of company car and we have set ideas, we have no flexibility at that level of detail.

If I want a VW, and you want a BMW, at that level of detail all we can do is try to convince each other of our choices.

Only when we recognise it's about choosing a car will other makes of car enter the negotiation. It's then possible that we can agree on an Audi.

I would like to provide a scenario to demonstrate how chunking up finds agreement.

Let's imagine you are working with two directors who are in conflict:

The sales director wants shorter lead times to deliver to the client quickly.

The operations director wants more time to manufacture.

These would seem to be bi-polar opposites. These people have fundamentally different opinions and will never agree. It's likely that it would be difficult to get them to talk in an agreeable way.

Let's see what happens when we chunk them up:

The sales director wants shorter lead times to deliver to the client quickly.

What's the intention? – To win business.

What's the intention in winning business? – More sales.

What's the intention in more sales? – Successful business.

The operations director wants more time to manufacture.

What's the intention? – Better quality control.

What's the intention in better quality control? – Customer satisfaction.

What's the intention in customer satisfaction? – Successful business.

By chunking up a couple of levels, we find that they want the same thing; they are just disagreeing about how to get it.

Making them aware of these shared intentions by chunking will not make them agree, however, it will change perceptions about the disagreement, they will be less rigid and more understanding about current behaviours – they can begin to negotiate.

When you chunk up, the 'topics' become more universal, less specific and more agreeable. Having a shared intention negates the possibility of conflict – disagreements will still exist but they become more agreeable and more workable.

A Negotiation model

The following negotiation model utilises chunking and framing skills to guide a negotiation from start to agreement.

1.   The first stage is to gain an agreement to negotiate – An effective pre-frame can be used to set out the parameters of the negotiation and introduce some flexibility.

2.   When the individuals involved have agreed to enter into a negotiation, chunk them up to a more agreeable perspective. Elicit a list of the things that are important to each party using questions, "what's the intention, for what purpose, what's important?"

3.   When you have the intentions and values at a higher chunk, gain a conditional agreement – as long as you have X, Y, Z then will you be happy to explore the options? As long as the intentions are satisfied at a higher logical level, the individual will be more comfortable letting go of pre-conceived specifics.

4.   Having gained agreement, you can chunk down to more alternative specific options, maintaining agreement as you do. You can use linguistic presuppositions such as double binds as 'closing' questions to influence this process in sales scenarios.

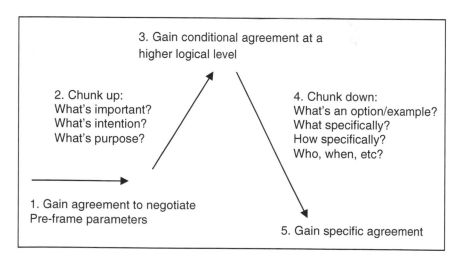

3. Gain conditional agreement at a higher logical level

2. Chunk up:
What's important?
What's intention?
What's purpose?

4. Chunk down:
What's an option/example?
What specifically?
How specifically?
Who, when, etc?

1. Gain agreement to negotiate
Pre-frame parameters

5. Gain specific agreement

The same model can be used for conflict resolution. Conflict takes place at a behavioural level – establishing the positive intentions of both parties breaks up the conflict, and then they can look for specific agreement together.

Let's run a couple of examples through this model.

Firstly a 'sales' style negotiation: Let's imagine a client is looking for a new accountant (and you offer that service).

Rather than assail them with your 'sales script' or talk about why you think they would buy your services, it would be more effective to find out what is driving their decision making process.

Having pre-framed the conversation in order to initiate the investigation, you can ask, "What's important to you about your accountant?"

The potential client, at this higher logical level, will provide values such as: pro-active service, specialism or experience in the same market sector.

You now have elicited their values. You may wish to qualify these, and you can gain a conditional agreement at this point. You could say, "I think my pro-active business has the experience and specialism to deliver the service you want. If I'm right, would you be prepared to work with us?"

Having gained agreement, you can talk about your service, using quotes and examples and matching it to the client's values, then asking more and more specific questions to 'close the sale' as far as possible.

Secondly, let's take disagreement involving two parties that want different things and see how we can employ this model to manage it:

Let's imagine that you need to mediate a discussion between two other people who need to select a new mobile phone for everyone in the company.

The two people have selected telephones and cannot come to agreement. They have done some research and are confident that their selection is the best for their requirements. Person A has selected a Sony Ericsson, Person B has selected a Motorola.

Simply urging them to look at alternatives will have little effect. They have already made a decision that they believe to be the best choice. You must first get all parties to agree to investigate. This can be achieved with an effective and agreeable pre-frame.

You can then begin to chunk them up – away from specifics and into values or intentions.

If you ask person A, "What's important about the Sony Ericsson?", they will provide you with their values that have led them to that decision. For example: Compact, with an MP3 player.

If you ask person B, "What's important about the Motorola?", they will provide you with their values that led them to that decision. For example: Slim and a flip up design.

You can now gain a conditional agreement: If we find an alternative that is compact and slim with an MP3 player a flip up design would it be OK to investigate the options available to us?

What's interesting is that, when you assure the individual that their values will be met, they are happy to let go of the specifics of the choice they have made. Without the conditional agreement of meeting their values they may remain inflexible.

Having gained this agreement, it's now a simple process of elimination, starting from all of the available items that fit that criterion.

Summary

To summarise the process:

- Gain an agreement that the flexibility to explore options or negotiate exists before you begin.

- Chunk up to elicit their values and intentions – in doing so you are creating more flexibility and more potential options.

- Utilise the values and intentions to gain conditional agreement.

- Chunk down, maintaining agreement to specific desired outcomes.

7. Presentations

School Days

Since becoming a trainer in the corporate world, I often think back to my time at school. I had a variety of teachers over the years and, thinking about it now, it's interesting how differently they behaved.

For example, I remember one particular teacher that just wrote on the board for the whole lesson and we were expected to copy down what was written, and we were then set tasks for homework. To me this was not teaching, but some pupils did quite well under these conditions. Another dictated entire essays. I remember the feeling of having gained nothing from the lesson except for a sore hand. I could go on; I remember one teacher that would set up experiments that he would demonstrate and we would then be expected to replicate them without any explicit instruction or explanation. Another would just provide theories and ideas without the 'nuts and bolts' of the theory in practice. The teachers I liked would introduce topics and encourage discussion and argument or set up contexts for us to discover what we were learning, creating our own examples and paraphrases of explanations.

Some years, I would change teacher and my grade would inexplicably drop, only to be boosted the following year with another change of teacher. I don't know if you ever had a similar experience...

I found this inconsistency frustrating at the time, and I thought it was me. I now understand what was going on a little better.

Teaching has certainly moved on since I was a child. There seems to be a greater awareness of learning and processing styles; and one would hope that leads to a greater degree of flexibility in how the information is put across. (I process a lot of information with my auditory rep system, evaluating what I have heard with A^R, and consequently spent most of my time at school being told to stop looking out of the window)

In addition to teaching styles, there's something else that makes an enormous difference:

I was recently speaking to a friend who is a teacher and was encouraged to hear his practical definition of what he considered to be good or bad teaching: He said something like, "Imagine that you are teaching Geography and the topic for the next day is farming; specifically crop rotation. The evening before the lesson you are revising and updating your lesson plan when you are interrupted by a

203

newsflash on your television relaying a major volcanic eruption or earthquake somewhere in the world. The good teacher is the one that deviates from the planned lesson in order to utilise the pupils' current interest and teaches about volcanoes or earthquakes." The bad teacher continues to teach about crop rotation.

Utilization

This is a key point, not only for teaching, but for any type of presentation. Can you imagine a musician getting half way through a track saying, "Everybody stop – I lost track of where we are, sorry, can we start again?" The only way to keep the audience engaged is to play on...

Imagine a stand-up comedian that ignores heckles and pretends that they are not happening. It would not take long for this to break the comedian's spell of laughter over the audience. If not utilised and turned into a gag, heckles become a distraction and undermine the comedian.

When you present there are a multitude of things that can happen from environmental conditions to unexpected reactions from the listeners. If you ignore these things and carry on regardless, you will lose the engagement of the audience.

I would encourage you to welcome the unexpected, these are the things that make your presentation alive and engaging if utilised correctly. If ignored they are a distraction to your audience and, more importantly, to you.

You can only lose control of a presentation if you are being controlling in how you put the information across. If you are completely flexible it is not possible to be undermined.

In addition to that, referring back to the Milton model, you can use whatever is happening to pace the listener's experience. Think about the effect of that for a minute.

Not my style

We know from previous chapters that people are different and they have a different representation of the world.

In addition to that, we seem to have different ways of processing the information we receive – different information processing 'styles'.

So, that in mind, here's how it all goes wrong: We have a tendency to explain things in the way that we understand them ourselves…

You will communicate from your own information processing style, and that may be different to someone else's. You explain things in a way that makes sense in your world – another person may require different information to understand.

In earlier chapters we have covered the linguistic patterns of influential speech. In this chapter I would like to add to these influential speech patterns by addressing how you can structure your messages to satisfy the learning styles of the entire audience.

We will be working from the assumption that people, when presented with new information, will be asking different questions. For now, it would be a good idea to create an example message to use as you work through this section; something that you need to explain or persuade someone to do.

What are they thinking?

Below is a simple model of the questions an audience will need answering based upon the 4MAT System developed by Bernice McCarthy.

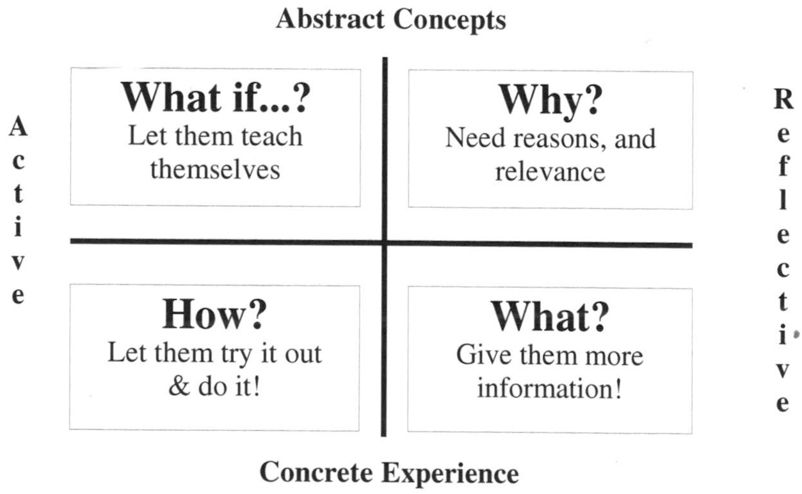
Abstract Concepts
What if...?
Let them teach themselves
Why?
Need reasons, and relevance
How?
Let them try it out & do it!
What?
Give them more information!
Active
Reflective
Concrete Experience

It's obvious from experience that we learn in different ways, and without quoting statistics or isolating people into one type or another, I'm sure that you can accept that we require different information to satisfy the different questions that we are asking at the time.

Someone thinking 'Why?' will be looking for reasons and relevance. They will be asking questions like: Why are we looking at this? Why is this happening? Why are we here?

Someone thinking 'What?' will want explicit information, and as much of it as possible. They will be asking questions like: What exactly is this? What exactly is involved?

Someone thinking 'How?' will want to know how it works, preferably by direct experience. They will be asking questions like: How does this work? How will it happen? How are we going to do it?

Someone thinking 'What if?' will like to experiment with results or consequences. They will be asking questions like: What will happen as a result of this? What if we do it this way? What if we don't?

We tend to present in a way that answers the questions that we ourselves normally ask. We sometimes even answer questions our preferred way rather than the way the question was asked.

For example:

Question: "**Why** are we moving office?"

Correct answer: "Because our lease has expired and we are 'cramped' in this building." (why? – reason)

Incorrect answer: "Because if we do we will have more space and a better location." (what if? – consequence)

Or alternatively:

Question: "**What** is this new system?"

Correct answer: "It's a new system for recording CRM information." (what? – explicit)

Incorrect answer: "You can use it to log and view customer information." (how? – process)

The first step in recognising these differences and utilising them, is to answer the question that you have been asked, rather than answering any question in your preferred style.

How can you talk to everyone?

The following table contains suggestions of how to present information in a way that will engage all of the previously described personality types.

Read the table below, and then begin to structure your message to fit into these descriptions:

WHY?
Pre-frame the communication: Tell story that explains why or explicitly share reasons. **Ensure that you are communicating positive INTENTION**
WHAT? Explicit Frame: Provide precise definitions and access to more information
EXAMPLE IN ANOTHER CONTEXT Make your point in another context: They will evaluate the idea without prejudice and be easily convinced
HOW? Context for discovery: Provide demonstration and an opportunity for them to do it
WHAT IF? Provide expectations of, and an open frame to discuss, effects/results/possibilities/consequences

To demonstrate this I will use an example that I used in a training session. My colleague Ben and I have a habit of providing each other with unexpected challenges at every opportunity.

On this particular day he said to the room full of delegates, "This system is so convincing that if you give Daryll a difficult topic, he will prepare a presentation in one minute and then convince you of it." Thanks Ben. Fortunately, this is not an unrealistic claim, and we now add this demonstration as a convincer into every presentation training that we deliver.

The example I will use here was provided by a client in the travel industry; they asked me how to convince their Financial Director that all business travel should be first/business class when they currently fly stand-by.

Firstly, realising that the message will be rejected if asked directly, I pre-framed the conversation as an exploration of an idea. I said that I did not know the answer to this situation and would welcome the opportunity to explore potential solutions. (This obviously pre-frames the presentation in a way that will make the listener more flexible).

I then began by addressing the reason (WHY) for the presentation. I may have suggested that many of the staff were currently travelling stand-by and being 'bumped off' flights. The intention of the stand-by arrangements was to save money, and this was not being achieved when the consequences of opportunity cost, negative perceptions caused by arriving late and the negative mindset of the employee entered the equation. I may also have suggested that many staff were travelling long distances in uncomfortable conditions and then expected to go straight into a meeting and perform well. (This should provide adequate reason to discuss whatever follows).

Then I made an explicit suggestion (WHAT) – that all travel should be business class or first class. As I said it the audience recoiled, so I utilized it, assuring them that they were right; it sounded out of the question, and therefore they would be surprised to hear what follows. I went on to be explicit about the conditions of the travel; that it would be with a few select carriers with whom they could negotiate exceptional volume discounts. I'm not sure how many made up details I added in at this stage – obviously in a real scenario this explicit information would be genuine and accurate.

At this point they were still listening with interest and far from convinced, so I broke off into a story. I told them about my friend Richard who raises sponsorship money for young athletes. Richard had told me that the UK number 5 in the high jump is completely un-funded. He drives up and down the country to national athletics meets, in an unreliable car which often breaks down and he fails to arrive on time. To overcome this he had been travelling to the meet the evening before and then, unable to afford a hotel, sleeping in his cramped little car the night before and hoping to perform like a world class athlete the following day. I was amazed to learn that this is how we treat our top athletes in this country. If they are not in the top few that get funding, they get no funding whatsoever. (This example in another context will be directly applied to the presentation – but because the context has changed, it is more acceptable, allowing me to make the point without resistance.)

I would then go into detail about the reality of implementing this idea (HOW) and walk them through the process. They could approach all of their current carriers, negotiate prices based upon a commitment to a substantial volume of activity and they could put controls in place to ensure that the costs do not rise above expectations. Again this was a load of stuff made up on the spot, in reality I imagine you would be able to walk someone through the process of your presentation or demonstrate it.

At the end I suggested that the performance and morale of staff would be greatly increased and the business would certainly benefit from individuals being comfortable during the extensive travel that they undertake. (WHAT IF) I then opened a frame for questions.

Would this work in reality? – I'm not sure. It has certainly worked for me with a variety of subjects and in all training sessions where I have done this as a demonstration. The point being; you can begin to notice how influential this message has become simply by covering the subject matter 'from all angles'.

Obviously, for purpose of demonstration I cheat a bit – using plenty of Milton Model patterns and VAK sensory descriptions so the delivery is extremely hypnotic and paces the listener into a 'yes' mindset throughout.

The way we communicate affects perception and reception

In 1968, Robert Rosenthal and Lenore Jacobson conducted experiments that involved giving teachers false information about the learning potential of certain students in grades one through six in a San Francisco elementary school. Teachers were told that these students had been tested and found to be on the brink of a period of rapid intellectual growth; in reality, the students had been selected at random.

At the end of the experimental period, many of the targeted students exhibited performance on IQ tests which was superior to the scores of other students of similar ability and superior to what would have been expected with no intervention. In some cases such improvement was about twice that shown by other children in the same class.

The purpose of the experiment was to support the hypothesis that reality can be influenced by the expectations of others. Obviously this can be positive or negative depending upon the expectation. Biased expectancies can essentially affect reality and create 'self-fulfilling prophecies'. In the context of this experiment, Rosenthal predicted that, elementary school teachers may unconsciously behave in ways that facilitate and encourage the success of the students they believe to be brighter.

Knowing that you will be communicating your perceptions and beliefs through your body language, voice tonality and choice of words; how does your belief in the ability of others influence their performance? How does your perception of your message affect other people's reception of your message?

I invite you to play a quick imagining game with me:

Imagine yourself walking into a meeting of some kind that you are dreading: You expect it to be difficult, a battle of wills that is likely to descend into a heated argument. See yourself in this scenario and observe your behaviour – How are you walking? What else do you notice about your behaviour?

Now imagine yourself walking into a meeting that you are looking forward to: You expect it to be fun and creative with plenty of laughter. See yourself in this scenario and observe your behaviour – How are you walking? What else do you notice about your behaviour?

What dynamic are you creating as a result of those different expectations? If you prepare yourself for an argument you may be causing that argument – even though you are oblivious to doing so; and when it happens you may say something like, "I knew that would happen," or, "I told you so."

What's even more dangerous is that our beliefs become self-fulfilling prophecies. We will find evidence for what we believe, and miss evidence that falls outside of that frame of reference.

If you believe that the performance of a certain person is poor, you will notice all of the things that support that belief, and miss all of the things that contradict that belief.

And you do the same thing with beliefs you have about yourself. You will find plenty of evidence for the things you believe about yourself, that does not mean that they are true.

There is only feedback

Any day now my son will begin to attempt to walk. When I think about it now the corners of my mouth begin to curl into a smile, I get a warm feeling in the centre of my chest and hope that I will be there when he takes his first steps. I can imagine the scene now – my wife and I kneeling on the floor, facing each other and encouraging him to walk from one of us to the other.

But what if, after his first attempt to walk results in a stumble and fall, he decides that he is no good at walking and will not attempt to do so in the future? He thinks 'I'm not a walker – I tried and failed' and resigns himself to a life of crawling. Is this likely to happen?

The ability to fail is something we learn in later life. The only way to fail is to give up. If you don't give up, you haven't failed. You have simply learnt another lesson that will help you to ultimately succeed.

Every time my son stumbles, he is learning another lesson that will ultimately allow him to walk.

Did you learn to ride a bicycle without a grazed knee or elbow?

I believe Thomas Edison said: "I did not fail, I just discovered 99 ways how not to invent a light bulb."

Any negative feedback that you receive is only feedback. And, when you think about it, feedback is extremely valuable. Without it, what have you learned?

The first time I ever delivered a training session, I handed out feedback sheets and was delighted to receive 10/10 for every question I asked. I showed the sheets to my business partner, Ben, and he suggested that the feedback was not particularly good.

I said, "Are you mad? How could it be any better?" to which Ben answered, "What have we learned? What would we do differently next time? How can we improve?"

I particularly like this Boris Becker quote: "Feedback is the breakfast of champions."

The ability to take on board feedback, and do something about it is often what distinguished the excellent from the average.

I would ask the question: Is it realistic to get everything correct on first attempt? I think not. Generally speaking there is a degree of trial-and-error in our learning process.

In order to develop we need to 'have a go', identify the errors we make, and do something about them so that we can succeed the next time.

If we are inhibited by 'fear of failure' it may prevent us from 'having a go', or it may prevent us from acknowledging the feedback we receive by attempting to defend ourselves from it.

It can be helpful to recognise that failure is not a permanent condition. If you reach the end of your life and insist that there are a few things that you have failed to achieve I may accept that. Until then; the only way to fail is to quit; to give up; to stop.

If you want to continue to improve, it is necessary to welcome feedback, and perceive it in such a way that allows you to treat it objectively, letting go of your 'defensive reactions'.

Without making what we perceive to be mistakes, we would be unlikely to learn anything new.

You can perceive feedback as criticism and retreat from it, or you can recognise feedback as the very thing you need to pay attention to if you are to improve; it's your choice.

Delivery

I hope that you are now ready to experiment with constructing influential and engaging messages.

Using the structure of the 4MAT system, you can add in Milton Model Patterns to make the presentation more agreeable and influential.

I would urge you to set conditions for yourself to utilise and incorporate whatever happens during the presentation to pace the audience experience, keeping them engaged and maintaining agreement.

To engage the listener even more, vary your voice tone, act out what you are explaining with confident gestures and add a variety of visual, auditory and kinaesthetic descriptions.

8. Self Application

Re-visiting the map...

Several years ago I was working in my office early one morning when a member of my team (who was often late) arrived early.

Surprised to see him I asked, "What brings you here so early; an accident in bed?"

He said, "Well, it's funny that you ask. When I began working here five years ago I experimented with several routes to work. I tried different roads at different times and discovered the best route to work. I have been driving to and from work the same way ever since. There have since been four sets of traffic lights and three roundabouts installed on that route, and it's taking half an hour longer to get here every day. Regardless of this I've still been using the same route to work, out of habit. I didn't give it any thought.

I was late for work twice last week so I finally revisited the map and realised I have been using what is now the slowest route to work. I have wasted hours without realising that I was doing so."

We can start again!

Today is the first day of the rest of your life. What will you decide today that will improve your journey? What have you taken from this book?

By now I would expect you to be becoming more and more aware of the many things that happen in our 'worlds' when we interact.

If you have managed to develop enough flexibility to experiment with new beliefs and perceptions, the Big Ideas in this work book should have provided you with plenty to re-evaluate.

In addition, your awareness of language and body language may well have begun to change to some degree.

One of the common practical applications of NLP is goal setting. In fact, of the many incorrect explanations of NLP that I have heard in the past, there have been some people who think NLP is goal setting. I found that perception amusing and confusing.

Well, certainly there are a couple of things that you can do to make your objectives more compelling in your own mind. To set up goals in such a way that it is almost as if they become a neurological filter of some kind, drawing your attention to anything that will support the achievement of that goal.

I'm not a fan of setting goals, or any other pattern that's full of conscious content, for reasons that I will go into later. However I appreciate that, for many people, this is useful so I am happy to run through an effective goal setting model.

For some reason or another you have picked up this book. I don't know if it's part of your Practitioner Certification, as an introduction to NLP or to gain just a few extra resources. Either way, there is an intention of self development on some level.

So I would like you to ask yourself a couple of questions. Take as much time as you need to reflect upon these: What is it that you want that you have not got at the moment? What is the outcome that you want for yourself as a result of your current development activity? Make a note of you desired outcomes.

Now that you have identified to some degree what it is that you want. We can run it through a goal setting model and make it a compelling and realistic outcome.

So where do you think you're going?

This section of the workbook can help you to achieve your goals if you know what they are. As you begin or continue your journey, you may end up 'going to the moon', which is great – if you wanted to go to the moon. If you really wanted two weeks in Disneyland you are going to be disappointed.

Why does having a defined goal make a difference? Every day you are confronted by choice of behaviour. Do this or do that. Write an email or make a phone call, contact one person or another, talk about a familiar topic or start a new one. Do it now, do it later or ignore it completely.

The idea is: if you have a clearly defined and compelling goal, it sets up a neurological filter or frame of reference that makes it very easy to make these micro decisions on a daily basis and end up in the place that you want to be.

If you do not have an overall awareness of where you are going, you make every decision based upon the presenting factors there and then, without an awareness of an overall direction. You may well make good decisions, but you will have no idea where those decisions are leading you.

Sometimes the small decisions we make today can make a big difference to us tomorrow.

How will you know when you get there?

When you decide to set goals you should really make sure that you do it well. A goal that is too easy does not drive you to perform. A goal that is too difficult may leave you feeling defeated, and that's not much of a motivator either.

How can you set the right goals? Have a think about it. What are your goals? **Firstly, state what it is that you want** (as per the previous page).

Then ask yourself why you want it; what is the purpose of that objective? It helps to be aware of the positive intention behind your goal or outcome.

Then identify, in real terms, exactly what you will do when you have reached the objective and state that as a positive outcome.

Do you remember "Don't think of baked beans"?

If you set a goal that includes the words 'don't', 'won't', 'can't', 'shouldn't', or 'mustn't', your unconscious mind will focus on the statement that follows them as if you had used the words 'do', 'will', 'can', 'should' or 'must'.

For example, if your outcome is, "I won't eat chocolate." This is ineffective for two reasons. Firstly, each time you remind yourself of your goal you are reminding yourself of chocolate. Secondly, you do not know what to do instead. There will be a positive intention in eating chocolate, and without an alternative behaviour, this intention is unsatisfied.

You may be creating these goals consciously at the moment, but as soon as your conscious mind becomes occupied with the next thing you will be revert to the behaviours that are outside of your conscious awareness.

Another thing that will make your goal more compelling is making it 'toward' rather than 'away from'. For example, more free time rather than less time at work, easier rather than less difficult, more focused rather than less distracted.

Secondly, make sure the goal is specific.

219

"I want more money", is not a good goal. All you have to do is find some change down the back of the sofa and the goal is achieved. Hooray! Be careful with intangible goals like, "more free time". How much free time exactly? What do you need to do to make this possible?

The goal needs to be measurable so that you can know when you have achieved it. What exactly will need to happen to know you've got it? Will you need to see a report? Will someone have to tell you? Will you be handed something? Think about exactly how you will know when you have it, even consider whether you need to see, hear, smell, taste or touch something.

Thirdly, make sure it is achievable. By all means aim high, just make sure it can be achieved and make sure it's realistic. Do you have the resources that you need?

When are you going to achieve it? That's an important question because a goal that 'rolls over' indefinitely is not a goal, it's a dream. Goals are meant to be achieved, and to ensure that you do, you need to know when you are going to achieve it.

To avoid disappointment, make sure it's just about you and does not rely upon anyone else, or any other circumstances that are subject to change. It really needs to be just about you because that's the only way you can be absolutely sure that you can make it happen.

Lastly, just check something: Is it really OK with you to set this goal? If you do what it takes to achieve it, will any other area of your life suffer? Will it take important time away from friends, family, relationships, community, self development, fitness or hobbies?

I'm quite sure I could double my earnings next year through increased work activity if I didn't mind the resulting divorce and expanding waistline. I would mind those things very much so double my earnings through more work activity is not a good goal for me.

Remember this checklist:

Positive	– Is it towards what you **do** want?
Specific	– What exactly?
Measurable	– Will you know when you have it?
Achievable and Realistic	– Can it be done?
Resources	– Do you have/can you get what you need?
Time	– When?
Self initiated	– Is it solely down to you?
Ecological	– Is it OK with all areas of your life?

To check the ecology of your goal, I suggest that you check it with the application of Cartesian Co-ordinates below: Rather than attempting to answer these questions, simply think about the questions carefully:

- What will happen if you do?
- What will happen if you don't?
- What won't happen if you do?
- What won't happen if you don't?

Now to make your goal or outcome compelling: **Make it real.**

When you have set your goal, it will help you to clearly imagine it happening. Create a realistic representation in your mind of your achieved goal.

Where will you be? Who will be there? What can you see? What can you feel (externally)? How do you feel (internally)? What can you hear? Are there any smells or tastes?

Now capture that experience – imagine taking a larger than life photograph in your mind with all of the sounds and feelings included.

Now imagine 'putting' the experience in all its detail into your future. Actually place it into the physical space around you so that when you look to the future the picture is there – something that you are looking forward to.

How achievable does it seem now?

Watch out for the story teller...

I have included the above content on goal setting because it is my perception that many people expect a practical book on NLP to contain some information on setting compelling goals, and it certainly works in my experience. The method outlined above will indeed make your goal compelling, and I would invite you to consider a couple of additional factors about goals. Goals are, by nature, a limitation.

Setting a compelling goal sets up a frame of reference in your mind that allows you to notice and utilize everything that will move you closer toward achieving it. Even really ambitious goals, when you set them up in a compelling way, will limit you because they may prevent you from noticing or achieving anything that falls outside of that frame of reference. Compelling goals backed with a lot of motivation and determination can create 'tunnel vision' in the awareness of the individual.

I would urge you to consider the consequences of devoting a large amount of your attention to the pursuit of just one thing.

I am often interested, and mildly amused, by perceptions of what constitutes 'success'. Like any nominalization the definitions vary widely and change from one context to another. There is, however, an underlying theme amongst many of the people I work or interact with.

To illustrate this kind of perception I would like to share a story: I was in a coaching session some months ago, and my client began to describe an individual that they held in high esteem. For the purpose of this story, let's call him 'Fred'.

The conversation was frequently drawn back to what Fred had achieved; what Fred said; how successful Fred was; how financially wealthy Fred was. I paid some attention to what the client was telling me about Fred and his success because, from calibrating on behaviour, I was able to observe some states in my client.

It was much later in the session that the client began to add in additional details about successful Fred. It transpired that Fred was suffering from several physical ailments that were essentially stress-related, was on his second marriage after an acrimonious split from his first wife and currently had no contact with his children.

Such comments usually pass me by without acknowledgement unless I can see by a visible shift in state that it is somehow significant to the client. On this occasion, I must confess, I completely lost my state. I stopped observing the client for a moment and found myself in my own thoughts, thinking, "What? This guy is your model of success? Are you kidding?"

I would like to make it clear that I am not making a value judgement about divorce or any other circumstance that an individual can so easily find them self in. I am making a comment about balance, bias and consequence.

The other thing to be aware of when setting goals is that, the things that we decide we want as a result of our conscious reasoning may not be the things we want at all. We have a terrific ability to 'tell ourselves stories'.

A huge number of us believe that a lottery win would make us happy. If this is your belief, I would urge you to look into any of the research into the links (or indeed lack of them) between a lottery win and happiness. It may negate your financial difficulties, and this will not automatically transform your state into one of permanent joy.

If you are interested in happiness or positive psychology I would point you in the direction of Martin Seligman at the University of Philadelphia. His books *Learned Optimism* and *Authentic Happiness* are very accessible.

In terms of setting goals to make yourself happy – be careful what you wish for......

As for what you can do instead, I would recommend that you set your objectives at the higher logical level of intention.

As we covered in the chapter on negotiation; at a higher logical level you have far more choices and options available to you. If you set very specific goals you are working at a lower logical level where the specificity is likely to be a fairly restricting, creating an outcome without much flexibility around how you can achieve it.

For the purpose of illustration, let's take the lottery win example. If you set the goal of winning the lottery you have one acceptable outcome – and an extremely unlikely one.

If you address the intention in the lottery win you will have far more flexibility, options and choice.

If the intention is to be financially independent, and you recognise that as the outcome, how many more ways are there of achieving that? What plans can you make?

If the intention is to retire, what's the intention in retiring? What would retiring get for you? More leisure time? More quality time with family and friends? Doing what you enjoy? If that's what's really important, how else can you achieve those things without retiring? What other options do you have?

I could go on. Whatever your desired outcome, ask yourself, what's the intention in that outcome?

If you set the intention as the desired outcome you will have far more choices and options about how you can achieve it.

Another Point of View

One of the techniques that is a prerequisite to any activity that could be called NLP is the ability to dissociate from your current experience. It's amazing how empowering it can be to step out of your immediate experience and gain a different perspective.

This different perspective is referred to as taking a different perceptual position. I will cover the three perceptual positions in this chapter:

Firstly, first position.

This is your experience of the world, looking out through your eyes, seeing what you see, and having all of the other sensory experiences like sounds and feelings.

You will remember many of your past experiences this way, as if you are actually having the experience. Some imagined experiences may also be seen from this perspective and are likely to contain feelings and other sensory information.

When you are experiencing your experiences in this way, you are associated. You are having the experience, whether real or imagined. Are you with me so far?

As human beings, we have the ability to disconnect ourselves from the first person experience. We can view things from another perspective in amazing detail. We can imagine what it would be like if we were viewing ourselves from outside, like an observer.

Second perceptual position is associating into the perspective of someone else; to view yourself as someone else would view you, which can reveal some interesting things about yourself, and indeed gain further insight into that other person's point of view.

This can be great for breaking down misconceptions and mind reads about other person's intentions or behaviours. For example, I occasionally have the opportunity to coach people through the interview process. In many cases people approaching an interview see the situation from their own frame of reference and, in the absence of thinking about the interviewer's perspective, make the mistake of 'mind reading' that the interviewer is there to be overly critical or 'catch them out'.

Think about this for a moment, if you were interviewing to fill a job position, would you hope to reject every candidate? What a waste of time that would be. So what would your intention as an interviewer be? Surely you would be hoping to find someone that you are happy to employ; you would be hoping that the applicants do well, wouldn't you? So what are you as the interviewer looking for? What is going to make the difference between similarly qualified applicants? What will sway you?

Without going into further detail of this application, I'm sure you can begin to appreciate that taking second position can be extremely resourceful for breaking up your unhelpful misconceptions and creating a more realistic and balanced perception of the situation you are walking into.

Third position is to dissociate from the situation and view it as a 'fly on the wall'.

Taking third position, so that you can see yourself as an impartial observer removes the emotion from the representation and allows us to evaluate ourselves free of any unhelpful shifts in state.

If you would like to experience this; first think of something you strongly like or dislike and create a representation of it in your mind viewed from first position – looking from your own eyes as if you are actually experiencing it.

Notice the feeling that you are having with that representation.

It may help to stop for a moment and do this with your eyes closed.

Now create the same representation but this time view it as the impartial observer. Make sure you can see yourself in the representation with the subject of the representation.

Notice the feelings have changed with that representation.

Again, stop and do this with your eyes closed.

The ability to create this impartial perspective is extremely valuable to us. If you are associated (1st position), you are likely to run the same patterns you have always run, and if you always do what you have always done... guess what.

Let's imagine that there is a situation that you find stressful, to which you have a knee-jerk reaction that is unhelpful to you. If you think about this past behaviour and create a representation from 1st position, you will get the stressful feelings and begin to think the same unhelpful way again. You are unable to gain a realistic perspective on your behaviour because you are 'in it'.

In order to generate choice and flexibility, you need to think about the situation without having the stress reaction, and taking the dissociated 3rd position will allow you to regard the situation without the overpowering emotions. At last you are free of the old pattern of behaviour and you can begin to think of alternatives that will be better for you.

If this book has provoked you to question your past behaviours and review them with a different outlook, or evaluate your current behaviour to look for possible improvement, then I would recommend that you view these scenarios from 3rd position with the intention of generating alternatives.

What prevents you?

Setting compelling goals is all a good idea in principle and it does beg the question why have you not done this already, what's getting in the way? Whatever that is; will it sabotage your future efforts?

There are a few things that you can do to make yourself aware of your un-resourceful thought patterns and the obstacles that you are putting before yourself:

Check your own attribution of meaning

Even when you are perfectly aware of the 'meta violations' of our surface level opinions, you may still finding yourself equating meaning to things.

We tend to learn by cause and effect – if I touch the hot oven it hurts or the appearance of the high-chair means it's dinner time; so the process of equating meaning to our experience of the world can be a hard habit to break.

When we begin to use this process of thought to apply meaning to the motives or opinions of others, it's pretty clear that these are nothing more than distorted 'hallucinations'.

I would remind you of some examples that we used in the investigative listening section where the speaker has used cause & effect reasoning or added meaning incorrectly:

"I know what they are thinking." – "If we charge more then the client will go elsewhere." – "They left us waiting in the reception area; that means they are annoyed with us."

This is meaning that you are 'adding in' without evidence; it's unqualified, a perception, a product of your imagination, a hallucination.

When you become aware of yourself using these thought patterns, challenge yourself. Does it really mean that? How do you know?

If you insist on creating hallucinated meanings, then hallucinate three times. Having created one possible meaning, go on to create two more. It is remarkable how empowering this flexibility of 'meaning' can be, and it will prevent you from running the same un-resourceful thought patterns.

Question your own modal operators

One of the clearest indications of inflexibility is a modal operator of impossibility (can't, won't), necessity (must, have to) or negative necessity (mustn't).

When I am coaching, if I hear one of these modal operators I immediately challenge it before anything else.

If I hear myself using one of these it 'stops me in my tracks'. Before continuing with whatever I am thinking or saying, I first challenge the modal operator that has appeared in my speech or thoughts.

The rules and boundaries that we apply to ourselves are often the very things that limits us.

When you hear yourself say 'can't' ask yourself; if it is really impossible? What prevents you?

When you hear yourself say the word 'won't', ask yourself: is there really no way?

When you hear 'must' or 'have to' ask yourself; what would happen if you didn't? When you hear 'mustn't' ask yourself; what would happen if you did?

Add options

A problem is only a problem because you have either become inflexible about how you deal with something (you only have one strategy for doing something, and when that strategy is ineffective or produces negative results, it becomes a problem) or you have become inflexible about a potential outcome (you have only one acceptable outcome, and if things aren't going that way it becomes a problem).

A problem ceases to be a problem when we recognise the choices we have.

Think about it; anything you currently see as a problem, what are you being inflexible about; what do you need to let go of in order to move on?

One choice is no choice; two choices is a dilemma; only with three of more choices are we really acting at choice and therefore 'at cause'.

The more you can add options (more than one way of going about things or more than one acceptable outcome) the more you can have flexibility, choice and influence over the results you get.

Listen to your own advice?

We discovered that: The way we communicate affects perception and reception. Let me take this idea a little further and suggest that your perception is a projection:

Imagine two people, let's call them Bill and Ben, talking about a mutual friend who has recently lost their job, let's call him Jack.

Bill says, "It's a nightmare, Jack is unlikely to find another job as good as the last one and he now has the agony of the interview process to go through."

Ben says, "Jack will be fine, the job market is booming and interviews are easy."

Bill and Ben probably think that they are talking about Jack, but the two contrasting opinions above tell us far more about Bill and Ben than they tell us about Jack.

Bill would have a nightmare with the interview process, Ben would be fine, and Jack is irrelevant – they are talking about themselves without realising it.

We have a tendency to put our stuff on other people.

The things that annoy you about others are a reflection of something you do not like about yourself. (Look at it this way – other people don't find the same things annoying as you do)

If it's pushing your buttons, you must have a button that can be pushed.

If you have some advice to give someone that is really annoying you – give that advice to yourself first. Just like stress, annoyance is something that you create. In order for someone to 'push your buttons', there must be a button to be pushed.

Coaching Behavioural Change

To provide just one more practical application of the patterns already covered in this book, I'm going to take you through a model for coaching behavioural change. It will be very effective if you apply the model to yourself as an evaluation of this process.

Firstly, like any communication, priming the conversation with an effective pre-frame will go a long way to negate defensive reactions and reduce the opportunity for misunderstanding.

If working with another person, they may not be aware of your positive intention unless you 'spell it out' to them. They may mind-read your intention as something negative and you can imagine how that will affect the dynamics of the interaction.

In coaching of this nature I recommend that you be explicit, open and honest about you intentions.

Bear in mind how influential your preconceptions will be in setting a frame for what you perceive and unconsciously communicate. Clean up your preconceptions to remove bias before you embark upon this process.

For example: "My intention is that you fully understand this feedback and that you are supported in making any positive changes."

Also, by separating your intent from the content, it will make it difficult for the recipient to 'shoot the messenger'. If the content of the conversation could be perceived as grizzly; you are not perceived as grizzly for delivering it.

I would also like to refer you back you the Big Idea: There is Only Feedback. The most effective way of negating defensive reactions so that the individual takes valuable feedback on board, is for them to perceive the feedback as positive – a grazed knee on the way to cycling competence. I would invite you to think of what story you would tell to effectively induce this way of thinking. This feedback is of value. Ignore it, deflect it or deny it and they are cheating themselves out of the very thing that will help them to improve and overcome their current challenges.

If your pre-frame is future focused, toward the positive changes that they can make this is far more resourceful than a reflective autopsy of previous negative results.

> **Effective Pre-Frame**
> *There is only feedback*

Having set an effective pre-frame, we are ready to begin: Now we need to address the feedback, or reason for the required change – and it is amazing how unqualified such feedback can be.

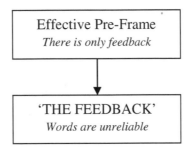

Remember: Words are unreliable! Meaning operates context-dependently. I was recently coaching someone that was given the feedback that they were 'arrogant'.

This is obviously some kind of nominalized value judgement and, as such, has no specific meaning so I asked him, "Do you know what you do that is arrogant?"

He said, "No."

I said, "Hmm, interesting, so would you know how to go into the office tomorrow and not be arrogant?"

He said, "No idea."

It's fairly obvious that this feedback is of little value. If the recipient cannot associate a meaning to the feedback, it's a criticism. It's of no use. How can they change something that they have no awareness of?

Similarly, process driven or numerical feedback can be equally useless. For example: If someone's 'numbers are down' in one area of the business, that's just a fact. It does not become performance feedback until we begin to get some idea of how it is happening or what events lead it.

Feedback is the observations of our actions; it does not provide an awareness of what the actions were in sensory detail.

So, from your awareness of how unreliable surface-level communication is, I'm sure that you can recognise that this feedback only becomes valuable when we qualify it.

My recent favourite piece of utterly useless feedback was, "You are not exhibiting management behaviours." What on Earth does that mean? When asked to specify the provider of the feedback said, "You know… management behaviours."

I would suggest that, if you are giving feedback that you cannot qualify, your input is more of a hindrance than a help to the development of that individual.

In order to get the individual to 'associate into' the feedback, you can ask them to provide specific behavioural evidence of whatever is causing the feedback using 'how' or 'what' questions and provocative paraphrasing.

For example: If the feedback is a perception that the individual is arrogant, you can ask, "What might you be doing that allows other people to create this perception?" or, "How specifically are you behaving?"

This should provide us with specific behaviours that the individual recognises they are doing. Now we have something to work with.

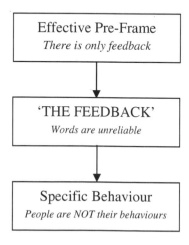

231

Resist the temptation to suggest alternatives at this point, any suggestions you make will be what you would do in their shoes, or what would be most effective for you. The person you are coaching is not you. They have different knowledge, abilities and intentions.

Having qualified the behaviour to work on, we know that 'People Are Not Their Behaviours' and that 'All behaviour functions from positive intention'.

Having established the relevant behaviour we can chunk it up to the intention behind the behaviour.

By the way; a 'not' behaviour is of no use to us. At any given moment there are a million things you are not doing. Right now you are not waterskiing. This is not helpful. We cannot discover the intention that is driving a non-behaviour. What is your intention in not waterskiing right now? We must first establish what behaviour the individual **is** doing that results in the non-behaviour.

Also watch out for mission statements. Intention in this context means intention for the individual. For example; something like: 'to deliver value to stakeholders' is unlikely to be intention behind the behaviour.

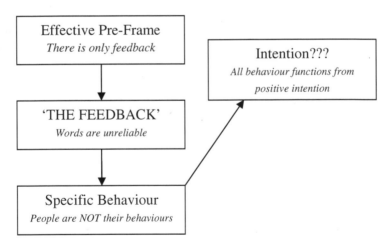

At the higher logical level of intention the individual has more choice and can clearly identify alternate ways of achieving the positive intention.

You can now assist the individual in selecting alternative behaviours that will be more helpful for them.

Unlike positive and helpful suggestions, or a logical, deductive thought process of conscious reasoning, they will apply the alternative because they satisfy the intention that is driving the current behaviour.

To work through this model, take a piece of feedback that you have been given and run it through this process.

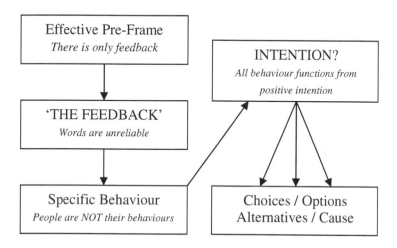

I would like to leave you with a last Big Idea that relates to the use of what you have learned with other people.

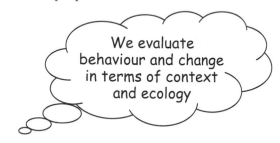

Have you ever come to an agreement with someone only to find they have second thoughts? Perhaps they will make things difficult, or back out of a deal.

From a practical point of view, if you effectively influence someone in a way that is not ecological for them, i.e. not congruent with their intentions, the influence will not be effective – if it is it will not last, and more consequentially, may have a damaging effect on your relationship with them.

If you are using these patterns in business, provided that you have an awareness of your positive intention and do nothing immoral or illegal then have fun with this stuff – from my perspective it's all just a game and we influence each other in commerce all of the time – that's what sales and marketing departments are there for. Just beware of over doing it.

If you are using these patterns in coaching, or any scenario when they are applied to the individual, then it is essential to evaluate any change in terms of ecology for that individual. Un-ecological changes may have more severe consequences.

Moving on...

So, just like the controls of a car during my first driving lesson, there is so much to pay attention to all at once.

Your ability to assimilate these communication patterns to a level of unconscious competence is unlikely without a substantial effort on your part. NLP is simple – it's not easy.

I would advise you to experiment, practise, play, observe, adjust and practise again. Be obsessive. Set yourself challenges. Isolate one pattern and use it until you have seen the effects and can utilise it easily. I wish you every success...

I hope that you have enjoyed this book.

As I look at this final draft on my computer screen I am unhappy with it. My experience and awareness of this material continues to expand, I could present this material so much better if only I could start again. There have been many changes already.

There comes a time when I must accept that this is 'where I am at' right now. Of course I can, and will, do it better tomorrow. By the time I finish typing each word it becomes a word that Daryll typed when he was younger and less experienced than he is now.

Whatever feedback this provokes, it's just feedback and is of enormous value on a continuing journey...

Bibliography

Authentic Happiness by Martin Seligman (Nicholas Brealey Publishing, Great Britain, 2003)

Blink- The Power of Thinking Without Thinking by Malcolm Gladwell (Little, Brown & Company, Great Britain, 2005)

Frogs into Princes by Richard Bandler & John Grinder (Real People Press, USA, 1979)

Patterns of the Hypnotic Techniques of Milton H. Erickson, M.D., Volume 1 by Richard Bandler & John Grinder (Meta Publications Press, Inc, USA, 1975)

Patterns of the Hypnotic Techniques of Milton H. Erickson, M.D., Volume 2 by John Grinder, Judith Delozier and Richard Bandler (Grinder & Associates, USA, 1977 – originally published by Meta Publications, USA, 1975)

Steps to an Ecology of Mind by Gregory Bateson (Published by University of Chicago Press, USA, 2000 – originally published by Ballantine Books, USA, 1972)

Structure of Magic, by Richard Bandler & John Grinder (Science & Behaviour Books, UJSA, 1975)

Structure of Magic 2, by Richard Bandler & John Grinder (Science & Behaviour Books, USA, 1976)

Science and Sanity: An Introduction to Non-Aristotelian Systems and General Semantics by Alfred Korzybski (International Non-Aristotelian Library Publishing. USA, 1958)

Screw It Let's Do It – Expanded by Richard Branson (Virgin Books Ltd, Great Britain, 2007)

The Seven Habits of Highly Effective People by Steven R. Covey (Simon & Schuster UK Ltd, Great Britain, 1989)

The Structure of Scientific Revolutions by Thomas Kuhn (University of Chicago Press, USA, 1970)

The Tipping Point by Malcolm Gladwell (Little, Brown & Company, Great Britain, 2000)

Tricks of the Mind by Derren Brown (Channel 4 Books, Great Britain, 2006)

Whispering in the Wind by John Grinder & Carmen Bostic St Clair (J & C Enterprises, USA, 2001)

Daryll Scott can be contacted at:

Use Your Noggin Ltd
Davidson House
Forbury Square
Reading
RG1 3EU

Tel: 0118 900 1527
Email: daryll@mynoggin.co.uk
www.mynoggin.co.uk